SO-DXN-429

Cases in
Business Decision Making

Education Development Center, Inc. (EDC)

David A. Garvin, Project Director, and
Associate Professor, Harvard University
Graduate School of Business Administration

Supported by the Exxon Education Foundation

THE DRYDEN PRESS
Chicago New York Philadelphia
San Francisco Montreal Toronto
London Sydney Tokyo Mexico City
Rio de Janeiro Madrid

Acquisitions Editor: Mary Fischer
Project Editor: Nancy Shanahan
Design Director: Alan Wendt
Production Supervisor: Diane Tenzi
Director of Editing, Design, and Production: Jane Perkins
Copy Editor: Nancy Dietz
Compositor: Impressions, Inc.
Text Type: Melior

Library of Congress Cataloging-in-Publication Data

Cases in business decision making.

    1. Decision-making—Cases studies. I. Garvin, David A.
II. Education Development Center.
HD30.23.C375 1987   658.4′033   86-29131
ISBN 0-03-009108-X

Printed in the United States of America
789-090-987654321

Copyright 1987 Holt, Rinehart and Winston
All rights reserved

Address orders:
383 Madison Avenue
New York, NY 10017

Address editorial correspondence:
One Salt Creek Lane
Hinsdale, IL 60521

THE DRYDEN PRESS
Holt, Rinehart and Winston
Saunders College Publishing

Cover Illustration: Mark Stearney

Contents

Preface   v

Acknowledgments   ix

Case 1   "So You Think You Know How to Run a
         McDonald's?"   1

Case 2   Think Volkswagen   21

Case 3   Milano Sportswear   37

Case 4   Gelateria Italia   51

        Gelateria Italia (A)   51

        Understanding Financial Analysis   56

        Gelateria Italia (B)   63

        How to Finance a Business   66

Case 5   Showdown at the Pioneer   75

Case 6   The Norton Company: Managing Change and
         Changing Management (A)   87

        The Norton Company (B)   101

        The Norton Company (C)   102

Preface

This book presents six original cases in business decision making, written specifically for community college classrooms. Instead of teaching business in the conventional way—as economic theory, a component of American history, or a set of basic skills such as accounting or data processing—the cases explore how business decisions are actually made: the issues managers and employees face daily, and how these decisions affect a company's organizational roles and responsibilities.

Each case is a narrowly focused document that tells a story, with people and a plot. It presents selected information that students can analyze and use to generate possible answers to the question, "If I were in that person's shoes, what would I do next?"

Designed to be modular, the cases can fit into ongoing courses. They can be used one at a time and in any order. You may wish, for example, to use just one in a course to illustrate in depth the concepts and issues you are teaching. Or the cases can be used as a series, introduced at different points in courses as varied as Introduction to Business, Marketing, Microeconomics, Operations, Finance, Business Policy, and Entrepreneurship. In addition, because the cases focus as much on analysis of information and problem solving as they do on specific business content, they have a place in nonbusiness courses as well. For instance, to give students a chance to "rehearse" making decisions in a complex world, philosophy instructors can use some of them in Practical Reasoning or Ethics. Other instructors can incorporate them into courses such as Allied Health, Legal Assistance, Psychology, Counseling, and Human Relations.

Cases, of course, are associated with the case method of teaching. That method is based on inductive, rather than deductive, reasoning. Cases do not present an abstract theory and then illustrate it with examples. Instead, each case provides a vehicle for discussion—a way the class as a whole can examine a particular situation and consider possible solutions. The instructor's role is to lead the discussion, show how the case links with other materials he or she is teaching, guide students as they discover possible solutions for themselves, and demonstrate how similar approaches can be applied to new situations. An *Instructor's Manual* with teaching notes is available to help the instructor adapt the discussion to the class' specific needs.

How did these cases come into existence? A few years ago I approached the Education Development Center with an idea and a question. The case method works extremely well with graduate stu-

dents in the MBA program at Harvard: was there a way to expand
the audience for this method of teaching and apply it in different
settings? EDC is a private, nonprofit organization. Begun in 1958, it
has a long track record of working with scholars and expert practi-
tioners to "translate" research and best practices into engaging and
useful materials. EDC was excited by the idea and suggested a partnership with a group that speaks for a particular universe of under-
graduates: the League for Innovation in the Community College. The
League is a membership organization of community colleges around
the country, encompassing 19 college districts, 53 campuses, and some
850,000 students.

The case method, we thought, had real potential for use in community colleges. Large numbers of the student population are adults
who have extensive life experience as workers, consumers, and learn-
ers. Many are enrolled because they seek retraining or re-education
to meet the demands of a changing job market. There are also students
just out of high school who will spend two years in college and then
move directly into the work force. For students in community colleges, the case method offers the opportunity to apply their own
knowledge and experience to real-world problems. And underpre-
pared students, also represented in some numbers, could respond to
the chance to show how they think through ways other than writing.

Together, EDC, the League, and selected faculty from Harvard
and Northeastern universities, with support from the Exxon Education Foundation, established the Alliance for Business Literacy Education (ABLE) and began to develop these cases. From the beginning,
faculty from League colleges collaborated in the project. They helped
to decide which cases to write, reviewed drafts, tested the cases in
their classrooms, reported on their experiences, and suggested mod-
ifications. The involvement of community college faculty, knowl-
edgeable about what kinds of cases would work in their classrooms,
has been essential to the success of the project. It has ensured that
the reading level, length, and complexity of the cases are suitable for
community college students.

The League faculty members were also keenly interested in
knowing more about the method itself. In a companion effort, supported by the Fund for the Improvement of Postsecondary Education
(FIPSE), U.S. Department of Education, ABLE is developing a training
package that includes a 60-minute videotape and a guide to teaching
with the case method and holding regional workshops for community
college faculty around the country.

We are very pleased to have The Dryden Press publish this case-
book; it is a major step toward our original goal of putting case materials into the hands of community college faculty members who can
use them in their teaching. Like most large projects, this one was a
collaborative effort. I would like to express appreciation to EDC Project Coordinator Cynthia Lang, Vice-President Cheryl Vince, and Pres-

ident Janet Whitla; to the Exxon Education Foundation for supporting
ABLE; to the advisory board members from education and industry;
to the faculty case writers who developed the cases; and to the "ABLE
Six"—the community college faculty who have been central to this
effort. Together they have created materials that community college
faculty can use as part of an innovative approach to teaching business
and problem solving.

David A. Garvin
Harvard Graduate School of Business Administration

Acknowledgments

Many individuals and institutions contributed to the development of these cases. Education Development Center, Inc., extends its special thanks to the following people.

EDC Staff
Janet Whitla, president
Cheryl Vince, vice-president
Cynthia Lang, project coordinator

The League for Innovation in the Community College
Terry O'Banion, executive director
Robbie Needham, associate director
Robert Kersten, St. Louis Community College
   at Florrisant Valley, Missouri
Robert Mellert, Brookdale Community College, New Jersey
Debbie Meyer, Brookdale Community College, New Jersey
David Stringer, De Anza College, California
Gerry F. Welch, St. Louis Community College at Meramec, Missouri
Mimi Will, Foothill College, California

Advisory Board
C. Roland Christensen, Harvard University
   Graduate School of Business Administration
Rose Ann Giordano, Digital Equipment Corporation
Harry Levinson, The Levinson Institute
William Wendel, Carborundum Center

Case Development Team
Kristina Cannon-Bonventre, Northeastern University
   College of Business Administration
David Garvin, Harvard University
   Graduate School of Business Administration
Alan Kantrow, *Harvard Business Review*
Cynthia Lang, Education Development Center, Inc.
Artemis March, Harvard University
   Graduate School of Business Administration
Michael Roberts, Harvard University
   Graduate School of Business Administration
Bert Spector, Northeastern University
   College of Business Administration

Education Development Center, Inc.
55 Chapel Street
Newton, MA 02160
(617) 969-7100

Case 1

"So You Think You Know How to Run a McDonald's?"

Developed by Dr. Artemis March, associate for case development at the Harvard University Graduate School of Business Administration, in collaboration with Professor David A. Garvin, Harvard University Graduate School of Business Administration, and Dr. Alan Kantrow, associate editor, Harvard Business Review. The cooperation of McDonald's Corporation and of the Arsenal Street store, assistant managers, and crew is gratefully acknowledged.

The Arsenal Street Store: June 7, 1984

Chuck Adams, owner of the Arsenal Street McDonald's, was beginning to wonder how many things he would be able to discuss at the meeting planned with his two first-assistant managers, Andy Maguire and Maria Costa, before he left to attend the local co-op meeting of McDonald's owners.[1] Since the Arsenal Street store manager had left three months ago, Chuck had been acting as manager.[2] He did not like to spend too much time at the store, though, because he didn't want to "shortchange my first assistants." Chuck commented:

Maria is very good at scheduling, and she does most of the ordering. Andy has a real knack with equipment, so he does most of the troubleshooting and minor repairs. All of that is included in the basic managerial training they've had here, and they go to Hamburger University for advanced training. Both of them are scheduled to go next year. They're both so good, I really can't promote just one of them.

Chuck had come over from his other store during the mid-morning changeover from breakfast to lunch. The changeover seemed

[1]All names in this case are fictitious.

[2]Owners had financial ownership of the store. Some owners also managed their stores. Some, like Chuck, hired others to run daily operations.

Exhibit 1.1   Personnel Violation Notice

```
                      PERSONNEL VIOLATION NOTICE


      NAME:    Frank Mathews
      DAY/DATE:  Wed, June 6, 1984        11:15 P.M.
      STORE:   186 Arsenal St.

      THE PURPOSE OF THIS NOTICE IS TO ADVISE YOU OF ACTION TAKEN BY YOUR
      EMPLOYER AFFECTING YOUR EMPLOYMENT DUE TO A VIOLATION OF COMPANY POLICY.
      THE VIOLATION(S) IS(ARE) THE FOLLOWING:

                     ( )  CASH REGISTER SHORTAGE

                     ( )  FAILURE TO REPORT TO WORK

                     ( )  EXCESSIVE TARDINESS

                     ( )  EXCESSIVE ILLNESS

                     (X)  OTHER (DESCRIBE)  Use of foul language
                              to crew member in front
                              of customers

      THE FOLLOWING ACTION HAS BEEN TAKEN:

                     ( )  WRITTEN WARNING (1ST, 2ND)

                     ( )  ONE WEEK SUSPENSION

                     ( )  TERMINATION

      CREW MEMBER'S SIGNATURE:

      STORE MANAGER'S SIGNATURE:

      SHIFT MANAGER'S SIGNATURE:  Eddie Clemente

      (ORIGINAL: PERSONNEL FILE          COPY: EMPLOYEE)

      FMC 109-010181
```

Source: Courtesy of McDonald's Corporation.

to be going smoothly except that one of the french-fry machines was not working. After trying a couple of things that didn't work, Andy had climbed up to the crawl space, found a broken belt, and replaced it.

Chuck looked over the messages on his desk. There was a Personnel Violation Notice (see Exhibit 1.1) from the night swing manager noting Frank Mathews had again been swearing at another crew member and in front of customers. This was the fourth violation on Frank's record, the second for bad language. Store policy was to fire employees for the fourth offense. Frank was a terrific worker when he concentrated on it. He could cook anything and handled "the bin"[3] better than almost anyone except Maria and Andy. Chuck knew that Frank was helping support his mother and younger brothers and sisters, and he was going to college part time. In the past, Maria had favored firing him, while Andy had wanted to give him another chance.

While Chuck was considering what to do about Frank, the phone rang in the manager's office. It was Dorothy Riley, saying she wouldn't be in as scheduled at 11:00 a.m. because she had a dental appointment. It was already 10:30. Dorothy had been working out well on the counter and with fries. As far as Chuck knew, this was the first time she had not shown up for work. He immediately had to decide whether to respond to her himself or call Maria to the phone. On today's lunch schedule he saw that the name of another crew member who also usually handled fries or worked on the Drive-Thru window had been crossed off. Chuck didn't know how Maria was handling that replacement. Had she found a breakfast worker who could stretch into the lunch hour? Had she already called other crew members to see if they could come in? What options did they have to cover Dorothy's absence? It looked as if Chuck might have to work a crew position during lunch. (See Exhibit 1.3.)

As the lunch pace picked up, Chuck noticed the milk-shake machine was leaking again. This was the third or fourth time in the past several weeks that it was oozing messily from the sides. If Chuck were to buy a new machine and also buy the equipment for the biscuits that the McDonald's Corporation wanted him to introduce, he would make a large dent in his equipment budget for the year. Two of his grills were six years old, and the company wanted store owners to replace equipment within seven years.

Moreover, reinvestment was one factor the company used to evaluate owners who wanted to expand, and Chuck Adams was hoping to open a third McDonald's store in the next couple of years.

The McDonald's Story

In the early 1950s, Ray Kroc, who was to become the founder of McDonald's, was selling a five-spindled milk-shake machine called a Multimixer. His curiosity was piqued when people from all over the country kept telling him they "wanted a mixer like the McDonald brothers have in California." Why, Kroc wondered, should people identify his Multimixer with a little store in the desert when he had been the product's exclusive distributor for 16 years? One reason was that the little store in the desert had not one or two but eight of these

---

[3]The bin was the holding area for finished sandwiches, located between the food preparation area and the customer counter. The person "on the bin" played a critical role in controlling what was made, for she or he noted the number and pace of customers, how many of each sandwich were currently made, and how fast each was going out. The bin person called out orders to the grill workers to make "12 burgers, please," or "6 Big Macs." Exhibit 1.2 shows the layout of the food preparation area.

Exhibit 1.2   Layout of Food Preparation Area

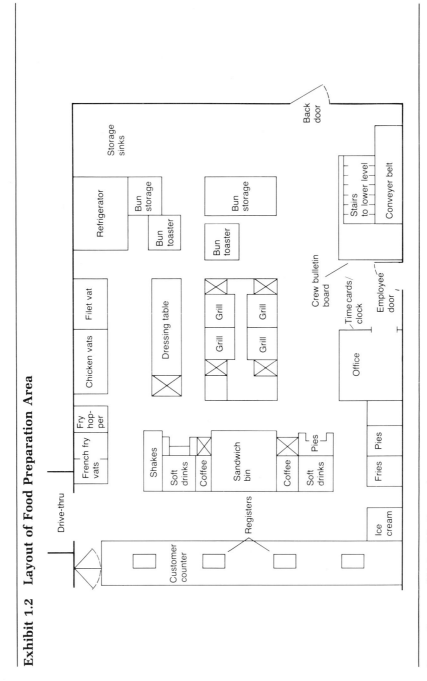

Source: Courtesy of McDonald's Corporation.

Exhibit 1.3 Crew Schedule

McDONALD'S TIME RECORD   WEEK ENDING _SUN, JUN 13 '84_

Name	Mon 4 IN	OUT	Tues 5 IN	OUT	Wed 6 IN	OUT	Thu 7 IN	OUT	Fri 8 IN	OUT	Sat 9 IN	OUT	Sun 10 IN	OUT	TOTAL HOURS
Amanda	12	5	11	5	12	5	12	5	12	5					
Dottie	8	11	8	11	8	11	8	11	8	11					
Maureen	1	5	1	5			1	5	1	5					
Paul	1³⁰	2³⁰	1³⁰	2³⁰			1³⁰	2³⁰	1³⁰	2³⁰	1³⁰	2³⁰			
Harry	6	2	6	2	6	2	6	2	6	2	7	CL			
Mary	7	2	7	2	7	2	7	2	7	2					
Carlotta	8	4			8	4	8	4	8	4	5	CL			
Jenny	10	2	10	2	10	2	10	2	10	8					
Joe	11	2	11	2	11	2	11	2	11	2					
Dorothy	11	3	11	3	11	2	11	3	11	3					
Carol	7	3	7	3	7	3	7	3	7	3					
Ellie	6	11	6	11	6	11	6	11	6	11					
Bob D.	7	12	7	3	7	3	7	3	7	3					
Andy	7	2	7	3	7	3	7	3	7	2					
Sally	8	3	8	3			8	2	8	2					
Jane	9	3	9	3	9	3			9	3					
Bill	6	10			6	10	6	10	5	CL	TRUCK				
Mark			6	10					5	10	5	10	3³⁰	8	
Vic							6	9ʷ					5	10	
Sarah	3	6³⁰							5	CL					
Tina											6³⁰	2³⁰	1³⁰	2³⁰	
Becky											9	5	7	3	
Joan			3	6			3	6	3	6	7	3			
Dave											8	4	9	5	
Debbie			3	6	3	6	3	6			10	5	8	4	
Barb	3	6			3	6			3	6			2	6	
Janet	5	CL	5	CL	5	CL					5	CL	5	CL	
Jack															
George	5	CL	5	CL			5	CL					5	CL	
Jank					5	CL	5	CL			5	CL	5	CL	
Jim					5	CL	5	CL							
Kathy					4	9	5	10			6	2	6	2	
Bob M.			3	7					5	10	5	10	5	10	
Nate	3	7	9	4					3	8	12	8	12	8	T
Cliff											1³⁰	2³⁰	1³⁰	2³⁰	
Nancy					3	6	3	6			7	3	8	4	
Pam			3	6			3	6			8	4	9	5	
Ginny	3	6			3	6					9	5	7	3	
Bobby	3	6							3	6	8	4	10	5	
John			3	6					3	6	10	5			
Mickey					6	10					6	CL	6	CL	
Evan	4	CL	4	CL	4	CL	4	CL							
Jeanne	6	10	6	10			6	10							
Ann			5	CL	5	CL			5	CL					
Archer	5	CL					5	CL	5	CL			5	CL	

Source: Courtesy of McDonald's Corporation.

machines. Kroc believed there had to be something more and decided to visit the store.

What at first looked to Kroc like an ordinary drive-in was actually a carefully tuned operation. "Each step in producing the limited menu was stripped down to its essence and accomplished with a minimum of effort," he observed.[4] Visions of McDonald's sprouting up all over the country—each with eight Multimixers—danced in Kroc's head. But the brothers were more interested in rocking on their front porch than in expanding their operation. Could someone else open the stores—Ray Kroc, perhaps? At 52, Kroc was sure that the best was still ahead for him, and indeed it was.

Thirty years later, in 1984, McDonald's opened its 8,000th store. While Wall Street cynics had claimed for years that the hamburger market was saturated, new units kept opening. Meanwhile, the average sales per store had risen to $1.2 million annually. Despite growing competition from Burger King Corporation and Wendy's International, McDonald's share of all the hamburgers sold in the domestic market continued to increase and now stood at 45 percent.

McDonald's Strategy

How had McDonald's done it? At first Ray Kroc thought that opportunity lay in selling Multimixers, but he soon identified an even greater opportunity: feeding a highly mobile population that ate on the run.

The first leg of Kroc's strategy was the careful choice of store locations. In the early days, Kroc would fly over suburban areas, count the number of schools and steeples, and then mingle with the people to get the feel of the place. In time, site surveys and market research became more sophisticated and thorough. But even after Kroc moved out of active operations and into the senior chairmanship, he retained control of site selection and continued to rely on his intuition. The company focused first on the suburbs, then on small towns, cities, and overseas locations. Most recently, McDonald's moved into sites where it can be the sole provider of food; it targeted hospitals, high schools, industrial parks, toll roads, museums, and military bases.

The second critical leg of Kroc's strategy was maintaining a limited menu, focused on hamburgers, french fries, and milk shakes. New products were added slowly, taking years to test. Some, such as the Big Mac and Egg McMuffin, were the suggestions of store owners. Breakfast fare was begun in 1976, an opportunity made possible by the company's use of grills for cooking hamburgers. Grills could be scraped down and their temperatures and timers reset during the changeover from breakfast to lunch. New product development was

---

[4]Ray Kroc and Robert Anderson, *Grinding It Out: The Making of McDonald's* (Chicago: H. Regnery, 1977), 6.

the second major area that Ray Kroc retained control of when he "retired" to the senior chairmanship.

Excellent sites and a focused menu were just the beginning. The entire operation was driven by Ray Kroc's motto: Quality, Service, Cleanliness, and Value (QSCV).[5] Kroc was determined to build repeat business based on the system's reputation rather than on the reputation of individual stores. That meant developing high standards and holding every store accountable for meeting them. Turning the QSC concept into action required a thick manual of standards and guidelines, as well as extensive training for managers and crew. Speed of service, for example, was identified as the critical feature distinguishing McDonald's from its competitors. The QSC form (see Exhibit 1.4) became a basic tool for store evaluation. High QSC "grades," given by corporate inspectors on visits to the stores, were necessary if an owner wanted to expand.

Company-defined standards controlled all aspects of the operations of a McDonald's restaurant. They determined product policy (what food would and would not be served), specified the ingredients of each menu item, dictated the equipment on which it would be prepared, and set forth the operations by which the food would be made—from the number of seconds a burger should be cooked on each side to the number of minutes it could be kept before being thrown out. No detail was too small to escape notice, and each was perfected. For example, meat patties were all beef with no hearts or fillers, contained no more than 19 percent fat, and weighed 1.6 ounces apiece.

The fifth leg of the McDonald's strategy was its franchise system, through which a minimum of 75 percent to 80 percent of the stores were leased to individuals who invested $300,000 to $350,000 to own and operate them. Kroc believed the vitality of the system depended upon the energy of these individual owner-operators, such as Chuck Adams, and developed the slogan, "In business for yourself, but not by yourself."

Company-Franchisee Relations

Over time, the company developed a division of responsibilities between itself and the store owners to whom it leased franchises (the franchisees). The company located possible store sites, bought real estate, and constructed the basic building. It then leased these buildings for 20 years to individual owners whom it had selected and trained. Current owner-operators and people who had been with the company for ten or more years were given preference in the selection process.

---

[5]"Value" was produced by Q, S, and C, so the acronym was usually shortened to QSC.

Exhibit 1.4   QSC Form

STORE _____ DATE _____ TIME _____ MGR _____ F/C–A/S ____

ADDRESS _____ Q _____ S _____ C _____

Value	Description
5 points — Designates excellence of performance	
4 points — Displays some deviation, but is acceptable	

Value	Description
3 points — These are values which denote unacceptability	
0 points — The difference of using a 3 or 0 is dependent on the severity of the problem	

93–100	points = A
85–92	points = B
77–84	points = C
76–Below	points = F

BREAKFAST ENTREES
OR LARGE SANDWICHES.

QUALITY

Big Mac – Quarters – Filet – Hot Cakes
& Sausage – Scrambled Eggs & Sausage. Test Product

	MEETS STANDARD	List of items purchased _____
STANDARDS	POINT	Price _____
		COMMENTS
Procedures: Amount & placement of condiments		
Holding Times: System being adhered to		
Overall Appearance: Proper package, neat, carmelization or toast		
Taste: Hot, fresh, moist		

	MEETS STANDARD	List of items purchased _____
REGULAR SANDWICHES: H.B.—C.B. or Egg McMuffin	POINT	Price _____
		COMMENTS
STANDARDS		
Procedures: Amount & placement of condiments		
Holding Times: System being adhered to		
Overall Appearance: Proper package, neat, carmelization or toast		
Taste: Hot, fresh, moist		

	MEETS STANDARD	Product purchased _____
FRENCH FRIES / HASH BROWNS	POINT	Price _____
		COMMENTS
STANDARDS		
Holding Times: System being adhered to		
Overall Appearance: Full bag/box, not greasy . . . good color and texture		
Taste: Mealy inside—proper salt		
Temperature: Hot		

	MEETS STANDARD	Item purchased _____
COLD BEVERAGES—SHAKES	POINT	Price _____
		COMMENTS
STANDARDS		
Proper Calibration and Taste		
Serving Temp. Ice, etc. . . .		
Appearance: Physical appearance of cup, amount, etc. . .		

	MEETS STANDARD	Product purchased _____
HOT BEVERAGES	POINT	Price _____
		COMMENTS
STANDARDS		
Proper Temperature		
Overall Appearance and Taste: Cup, marshmallows, proper condiments		

	MEETS STANDARD	Product purchased _____
DESSERTS/PIE/DANISH/SUNDAES/CONES	POINT	Price _____
		COMMENTS
STANDARDS		
Proper Weight: Texture, thickness, etc. . . .		
Holding Time: System being adhered to		
Taste and Appearance: Flavor, blend, color; neat		

TOTAL POINTS QUALITY SECTION		20 questions total 100 possible points

COMMENTS SUGGESTIONS

_____

_____

_____

_____

Source: Courtesy of McDonald's Corporation.

Exhibit 1.4 *continued*

SERVICE

This area is a mix of our service standards, customer convenience, and the appearance of our personnel. Presently it is weighed at 60% for quality of service and 40% for the length of time required during the actual "service experience" (basic steps). Twelve questions relate to this experience. They total 60 possible points. The time section offers 20 points for the standard of line time and 20 points for counter time.

Service	MEETS STANDARD POINT	Comments
Management Appearance		
Crew Appearance		
Greeting Customer		
Taking Order/Second Greeting at Drive Thru		
Suggestive Selling/Selling Up		
Assembling Order		
Presenting Order		
Receiving Payment		
Thanking Customer		
Conduct of Entire Crew		
Overall Pleasant Experience		
Customer Convenience Avail.		
Service Quality Total		

Line Time / Service Time	Prompt response at Drive Thru speaker (15 Sec.) Clarity of communication system	20 Pts		Please Check Appropriate Box: In-Store Visit / Drive-Thru Visit / Both
Counter Time	Drive Thru Window Time	20 Pts		If you choose to evaluate both drive thru and in store: 10 points should be allocated toward each.

Total	Quality of: ___ Speed of: ___ TOTAL		12 Questions at 5 possible points 60 points 2 at 20 Points 100 possible points

If a more thorough evaluation of service speed is required, complete the following section:

Customer	Time in Line	Time at Counter	Drive Thru	Comments
1.				
2.				
3.				
4.				
5.				
6.				
7.				
8.				
9.				
10.				
Avg. Time				
Standards				

Comments as related to solutions or goals from previous consultation:

Exhibit 1.4 *continued*

CLEANLINESS

Upon entry to the store take in the entire experience of cleanliness, in terms of how a customer would view it according to our standards. This section contains 20 questions valued up to 5 points each, total 100 points.

Exterior	MEETS STANDARD POINT	Comments
Approach to Store		
Parking Lot & D/T Pad		
Landscaping		
Trash Receptacles		
Corral		
Signage & Flags (Inc. D/T)		
Building Exterior		
Walks & Windows (Inc. D/T)		
Section Total		8 questions at 40 possible points

Comments as related to solutions or goals from previous consultation:

_____

_____

_____

_____

_____

Interior lobby/seating	MEETS STANDARD POINT	Comments
Seating—Decor		
Children high chairs		
Walls, Lighting, and Ceiling		
Trash Receptacles/Pest Control		
Restrooms		
Floors & Baseboards		
Front Counter		
Section Total		7 questions at 35 possible points

Comments as related to solutions or goals from previous consultation:

_____

_____

_____

_____

Interior kitchen	MEETS STANDARD POINT	Comments
Visible Work Stations		
Walls—Floor—Ceiling		
Stainless		
Center Island		
Menu Board & Display		
Section Total		5 questions at 25 possible points
TOTAL		20 questions total 100 possible points

Comments as related to solutions or goals from previous consultation:

_____

_____

_____

_____

_____

Even current owners, however, had to meet certain standards to be eligible for expanding. These standards included grades on the QSC form, reinvestment in the building and equipment, participation in the local owners' advertising cooperative, volume of business, and general attitude and involvement. Owners also had to be current with their creditors. Getting a new franchise became increasingly difficult. People who had been approved could be on a waiting list for two or three years. The company did not finance its owners. Every owner had to put up 40 percent of the initial cost from personal resources, without borrowing. (See Exhibit 1.5, Franchisee Start-Up Costs.)

For this investment, the owner got the right to occupy the premises and to use McDonald's trademarks, designs for kitchen and restaurant layout, and formulas and specifications[6] for menu items. The owner also had to use McDonald's methods of operation, inventory control, bookkeeping, accounting, and marketing. The owner received extensive and systematic training from McDonald's for operators, managers, and crew. Added benefits were shared national advertising and ongoing supervision and support from the field service staff. McDonald's research and development (R&D) group designed each piece of specialized equipment and then developed precise specifications for its manufacture. As a result, there were at most three manufacturers from which a store owner could buy a given piece of equipment. Similarly, R&D created new products and set specifications for the purchase of food and paper products. Since every McDonald's ordered the same ingredients, regional distributors emerged that could deliver to every store most of the food and paper products at a consistent quality and favorable price. (Unlike many franchisers, McDonald's did not get into the business of supplying its own stores. Kroc believed that trying to sell to stores at a profit contradicted his basic premise of an equal partnership with store owners.)

In return, the owners returned 11.5 percent of their net sales to the company in the form of rent and fees, and they were expected to be involved in community service. Stores were, of course, expected to operate in accordance with QSC standards. Every year the field service staff performed a three-day "full-field" review of each store and followed up with brief visits and QSC forms. Mandatory full-field reviews were suspended in 1983 because of owner complaints. However, an owner could still request a full-field visit, and, in Chuck's view, a smart owner would do so. High grades were necessary for the owner who wanted to expand, and Chuck, for one, felt more comfortable requesting a review than having to accept one.

---

[6]Specifications (specs) spell out precisely the limits within which all critical characteristics of a product must fall. Depending on the product, they are spelled out through chemical formulas, machine tolerances, percentages of ingredients that must be present or absent, etc. Specs control what may be purchased from an outside supplier or manufactured within the company; "setting tight specs" usually limits the number of firms that can meet the criteria.

Exhibit 1.5   Franchisee Start-up Costs

Conventional Franchise

The following represents the fees and approximate costs of a new McDonald's restaurant. Size of the restaurant facility, area of the country, and style of decor and landscaping will all affect costs. Forty percent of the total cost must be funded from non-borrowed personal resources. The remainder may be financed from traditional sources. McDonald's does not provide financing or loan guarantees, nor does it permit absentee investors.

Term	20 years.
Ongoing Fees	A monthly fee based upon the restaurant's sales performance (currently 3% of monthly sales) plus a minimum monthly fee, or 8½% of monthly sales, whichever is greater.
Initial Costs	

Initial Costs	
$12,500	Paid to McDonald's. Initial fee earned by McDonald's at the time the McDonald's restaurant is ready for occupancy.
$15,000	Paid to McDonald's and subject to refund. Interest-free security deposit for the faithful performance of the franchise, refundable at the expiration of the franchise.
$135,000	Paid to supplier. Approximate cost of kitchen equipment not including taxes, delivery, and installation.
$35,000	Paid to supplier. Approximate cost of seating and decor not including taxes, delivery, and installation.
$18,000 to $26,000	Paid to supplier. Approximate cost for taxes, delivery, and installation of the signage, equipment, seating, and decor. (Amount varies depending on state and local taxes, distance, etc.)
$10,000 to $31,000	Paid to supplier. Approximate cost of cash register system. The lower figure is for mechanical registers; the higher figure is for computerized registers.
$50,000 to $75,000	Paid to suppliers. Approximate cash requirements for miscellaneous equipment, franchisee's construction options, landscaping, operating cash, safe, first month's rent, training, preopening expenses, etc.

$298,500 to $352,500	**Approximate Total Cost.**

Source: Courtesy of McDonald's Corporation.

Owners were also expected to contribute to national and local advertising. They gave 2 percent of their net sales to national electronic advertising, while the McDonald's Corporation paid for the creative and production costs of these national ad campaigns. One of the earliest advertising creations was the clown Ronald McDonald, the cornerstone of the child-focused advertising that dominated until 1976–77. The serious side of the clown emerged in "Ronald McDonald houses," now numbering more than 60. Here families of ill children could stay at little or no cost while the child was hospitalized or receiving treatment far from home. Advertising and community service thus came together in the person of Ronald McDonald.

At the local level, store owners got together in a co-op to develop ads with their own agency. Chuck's co-op included about 200 stores in eastern Massachusetts, Rhode Island, southern New Hampshire, and eastern Connecticut. Contributions to the local co-op were running at a rate of 2.5 percent of net sales. Most went for Boston and Providence radio and television advertisements, with the balance going to the co-op's agency for creating and producing the ads. The co-op was pretty much on its own, although it often tied in with generic national campaigns. For example, if the corporation were pushing beef, the co-op might promote Big Macs. Individual stores ran corporate promotions as well as their own, using in-store materials or print media. Chuck Adams, for example, used print media, but only to promote new products. New products also meant up to $1 million in co-op advertising and could even raise the contribution rate by a fraction of a percent.

Store Operations

Every aspect of operations was developed and standardized by corporate headquarters. The job of the store manager was to make all the procedures and policies work in a particular store, with an ever-changing crew, in the face of all the things that could go wrong on a daily basis.

At the core of this activity was McDonald's system of food preparation and service. To ensure speedy service, McDonald's had chosen to "make-to-inventory": to make french fries, sandwiches, and pies ahead of a customer's order and to store them only briefly. To maintain quality, burgers were kept no more than ten minutes after they were made. To balance speedy service with quality and still not incur heavy costs because too much food was being thrown away, the amounts of each item put into inventory had to be constantly monitored and adjusted. How much of an item to stock at a given moment was a critical decision, one that had to be made and remade all day long. Although the corporation provided charts that indicated how much of each product to stock when sales were at a given level, many managers found the charts to be too rigid and believed there was no substitute for experience and having a "feel" for what was needed at the moment.

Deciding what to stock, and thus what to produce, was the responsibility of the person "on the bin." The bin was placed midway between the food preparation area and the customer counter (see Exhibit 1.2). Sandwiches were temporarily stored in chutes in this bin; each chute was for a particular sandwich (hamburger, cheeseburger, Big Mac, and so on), and each sandwich was held in a different-colored Styrofoam box or paper wrapper. The bin person called for the production of particular sandwiches ("Joe, 12 burgers, please"), listened for acknowledgment that the grill person had heard the order, boxed other batches of sandwiches called for a minute or two earlier, and marked the last of each batch with the time it should be thrown away. At the Arsenal Street store, Maria or Andy always worked the bin during peak periods such as the lunch-hour rush. The position was critical, because the person who worked the bin not only controlled the flow of products but also could keep an eye on everything that was happening in the store.

In addition to being paced by the call for orders from the person on the bin, crew work was paced by the buzzers and lights on the grills, the french fryer, and the filet fryer. It was directed by scheduled work assignments. Each person was assigned to a position for every shift for which he or she was scheduled: the grill, the Drive-Thru window, the fries, or the counter. During the peak breakfast and lunch periods, the tasks for a particular workstation were subdivided, and more people were added to the position. For example, during the midmorning hours, Cindy O'Connell worked alone on the Drive-Thru window. As lunchtime arrived, her job narrowed. She took orders, punched them into her computer terminal, relayed the total amount to the customer, collected the money when the car reached her window, and handed the order through the window.[7] Another person assembled the order, and still another "ran" between the order-maker and Cindy. Either Andy or Maria usually assumed the "runner" position, because it was a critical position from which to keep tabs on a great deal of activity. Cindy's video screen and a second video screen over the bin area both gave the order-maker the same information needed to put the order together. If the pace became extremely busy, the physical and financial exchanges between Cindy and the customers could also be subdivided, with a different crew member handling each exchange. As the pace slowed after breakfast and after lunch, these distinctions were eliminated, fewer persons handled each work station, and fewer persons were scheduled to work (see Exhibit 1.3).

The McDonald's production system, too, was highly interconnected. Each part of the sandwich assembly process had to be done at the same pace, or in balance. Otherwise, extra hamburgers would pile up, awaiting buns. Thus, workers whose tasks were interdependent—for example, the bun person, the grill person, and the bin person—had to work in synchronization with one another. In making hamburgers, Jenny Davis put 12 crowns (tops) onto a tray,

---

[7]People in cars gave their orders at the back of the store, then drove around to the side where they exchanged money for food through the Drive-Thru window.

which she then placed in a special bun toaster, while Joe Walters put 12 frozen patties onto the grill. While Joe seared and turned the patties, Jenny placed 12 bun heels (bottoms) on another tray and into another toaster and removed the tray of crowns to the dressing (condiments) table. Both workers dressed the crowns with condiments that squirted out in premeasured amounts. Joe then picked up the tray, hooked it to the edge of the grill, and placed the patties on the crowns two at a time. Just as he put the last two patties on the crowns, Jenny slid all 12 heels onto the patties in a single move. Joe then unhooked the tray and placed it on a shelf above the grill. In response to his cue "burgers up," Maria took the tray from the shelf, quickly wrapped the hamburgers, then put them in the chutes—all the while monitoring other activity and calling for other orders.

All these steps were carried out with little talk. Because the production system was so completely standardized and every person assigned to a position for which she or he had been trained, very little information was needed to trigger production.

Management and Crew

A McDonald's franchise with the volume of the Arsenal Street store employed between 50 and 60 crew members, 5 swing managers, 2 first-assistant managers, and a manager who might also be the owner. As owner, Chuck Adams handled advertising, community service and relations, and relations with the corporation and its field staff, and he decided on major purchases such as those for new equipment and store remodeling. He delegated as much as possible to Maria, who had worked for him for three years, and to Andy, who had worked for him for six years. At the same time, Chuck noted, "I am responsible for everything."

Maria scheduled the crew, using each person's general availability and taking into account each person's requests for time off. Her guiding principle was to schedule someone who was weaker at one position with someone who was stronger. Maria also did most of the ordering once a week. Everything but buns and dairy products was ordered from a single distributor that supplied about 500 McDonald's franchises in New York and New England. Of Maria's performance, Chuck said the following:

A couple of weeks ago, the whole grill system tripped out just before dinnertime, and we couldn't cook any meat. The system was down for a couple of hours before they could get it fixed. When I came in the next day and was looking at the sales receipts, there was hardly a dip in the total. The only way I knew something was wrong was that all the receipts read fish and chicken, no burgers.

Andy and Maria did most of the hiring and training of the crew. Maria described her hiring criteria as consisting of "how they come across," their references, and whether she could work them in or have someone work them in. The first assistants also oversaw the maintenance crew, maintained the supply of dry and frozen food products, and handled the cash. They saw to it that any advertising or promotional materials were correct and posted at the right time. In addition, Andy handled equipment maintenance and repairs that did not require an expert.

Andy and Maria were assisted by swing managers. The swing managers, who were paid hourly, assisted in running operations, opening and closing the restaurant, settling complaints with customers, sending crew members on break and seeing that they were back, and stocking kitchen freezers and refrigerators for the day.

Full-time crew, many of them women in their thirties and forties, often worked breakfast through lunch. High school students worked after school and part of the weekend. College students, people who held a daytime job, and married women who had small children tended to make up the nighttime workers.

Crew members received one-to-one training supplemented by videotapes for each station. The videotapes were staggered over a few months and included modules on burgers, fries, shakes, counter, breakfast, and all other areas of operations. Chuck Adam's policy was usually to start women on the counter because, he said, "they tend to be better with people," and then to begin assigning them to Drive Thru, fries, and shakes. He usually had men start on the grill and trained them to cook different things. This kind of "cross-training" of each person for several positions allowed greater flexibility in scheduling, in handling peak periods, and in dealing with absenteeism and employee turnover.

The McDonald's Corporation provided a five-volume management training course. Training covered all aspects of operations management, staffing, supervision, budgeting, basic accounting, inventory and quality control, equipment maintenance and repair, sales analysis, local store marketing, and community relations. By the time assistant managers went to Hamburger University at corporate headquarters, they were well into Volume 3. Hamburger U. was a sophisticated, modern center that provided advanced training through seminars, audiovisual presentations, and a model restaurant on the premises.

June 7, 1984

Chuck Adams had come to his Arsenal Street store to meet with Maria and Andy about recruitment and to get their reaction to the proposed new product, biscuits.

Recruitment was becoming tougher as the economy picked up. College students were now able to get other kinds of summer jobs,

Exhibit 1.6   Profit and Loss Statement

TARGET %	ITEM
100%	Net Sales
−35%	minus Cost of Sales (including food, waste, and paper)
65%	Gross Profit
−35%	minus Controllable Costs
	(including salaries, wages, payroll taxes, advertising, utilities, equipment maintenance and repair, and store maintenance)
30%	PACC (Profit after Controllable Costs)
−11.5%	minus fees to corporate (8.5% rent, 3% service fee)
− 5%	minus Other Expenses (including depreciation, taxes, interest, and licenses)
12%	Net Operating Income
− 2%	minus Owner's Fee/Bonus
10%	Net Income

Source: Courtesy of McDonald's Corporation.

and shopping malls were attracting the high school students with comparatively higher starting wages. If Chuck boosted his starting wage from $3.35 to $3.50 an hour, he knew he would have to raise the wages of his more experienced employees as well. Since he didn't think it would be possible to increase the wages of all his employees by 15 cents an hour, he had to consider the psychological effect of giving them smaller increases. Wages were already taking 17 percent of sales; an increase would cut into Chuck's controllable profits—unless sales increased as well. (See Profit and Loss Statement, Exhibit 1.6.)

Profit after controllable costs (PACC) was the income a store made after the costs that the manager could control were subtracted from the money brought in from the sale of food. Items over which a manager had some discretion about how much was spent—such as ingredients, food, and wages—were called *controllable costs* and also served as a measure of management performance. Chuck rewarded good performance with a bonus system that was based on holding controllable costs to 70 percent of sales, thus achieving a PACC of 30 percent. Bonuses were figured each quarter, and managers (or in this case, assistant managers) received 1 percent of the PACC. Chuck, therefore, had to consider the financial effect of increasing wages on his "bottom line," or PACC, an effect that was also of great interest to Maria and Andy.

Achieving a PACC of at least 30 percent could also be accomplished by increasing the volume of sales. Past experience had shown Chuck that higher profits followed from a higher volume of sales, and that attaining a higher volume of sales was more costly in terms of wages. He observed, "When I had triple-A ratings, I had the highest profits I ever had, and we were heavily invested in wages to do it." Therefore, Chuck was considering an alternative to raising the starting wage: the use of a dual rate. With this method, Chuck would pay a much higher rate—$4.75 or even $5.00 an hour—to all employees during the three-hour lunch period, when the store generated nearly 40 percent of its sales. This option had taken shape when Chuck found that the shopping malls were paying wages of more than $4.00 an hour, and it was becoming increasingly difficult to attract people to work for lower wages at that time of day.

In addition to making decisions about recruitment and wages, Chuck Adams had to decide what to do about a proposed new product. He had just received a letter from the McDonald's Corporation saying it wanted its New England stores to introduce biscuits in eight weeks. (See Exhibit 1.7) If a majority of the co-op stores voted for the idea, all the area stores would have to accept it. Chuck wanted to talk with Maria and Andy before the co-op meeting to discuss the implications for store operations, to decide which way to vote, and to determine the issues and questions he and other local owners wanted the corporation to address.

If the stores voted to introduce biscuits, they would be the second new product this year. Sausage McMuffin had been added to the breakfast menu just a few months earlier. McDonald's national marketing manager had told Chuck the company wanted to try biscuits in a northern market, and if the northeast region didn't take biscuits this August, he was not sure when they might get them. Chuck favored the addition of biscuits to his breakfast menu. He had heard from several southern store owners that the biscuits were terrific and knew they were boosting sales in those markets. But the timing could hardly be worse, because August was vacation month for some of the store's full-time crew. In addition, some of the college students who promised in June to stay until Labor Day invariably took a few weeks for themselves before going back to school. Chuck would have to hire additional staff to handle the anticipated increase in sales and also would have to find a baker, because the biscuits were put together in the store. He knew the additional equipment would cost about $7,000 plus installation fees, and he guessed co-op advertising could run to $1 million. There were many other operational implications as well, and Chuck wanted to think through with his first assistants what those implications would mean for the store. Could they all be handled in eight weeks?

Just then, when the lunch rush had eased and it looked as though Maria and Andy would be able to sit down and talk, Chuck heard the sound of a honking horn through the back door. He knew what that meant: The buzzer that went off when a car drove around the back of the store to place an order was not working, and Cindy had no way of knowing a car was waiting to place an order.

Exhibit 1.7   Letter from Corporate on Introducing Biscuits

June 1, 1984

Mr. Charles Adams
McDonald's Restaurant
186 Arsenal Street
Watertown, MA 02172

Dear Chuck:

We have selected the eastern New England area as the first area outside of the South to introduce biscuits for the breakfast menu. As you know, our southern stores have found it necessary to carry a breakfast biscuit to compete in their area. Our R&D Department has worked closely with some of our southern franchisees to develop a superb biscuit. Breakfast sales have already shot up 15 to 20 percent in these stores. (See attached sales data.)

We want to extend this opportunity to increase breakfast sales to our northern stores. We would like to have every one of the 192 stores in your area on-line by August 3, 1984, and to roll out a major co-op advertising campaign ten days later. While we recognize this rollout is much faster than what we have done in the past, we believe that with our support, you can do it.

R&D has developed a specialized biscuit oven, a holding cabinet, a convection oven, and count-down timer for this product. (Detailed equipment and cost sheet is attached.) This equipment is available from Jamieson Equipment.

Our corporate marketing team will be meeting with your co-op's steering committee on June 12 and 13 and with the full membership on the evening of the 12th. We will discuss all the issues and try to answer all your questions at that time.

Sincerely,

Don Hughes

Don Hughes
National Marketing Manager

Note: This exhibit is a fictitious example.

Case 2

Think Volkswagen

Developed by Cynthia Lang, senior associate for development for Education Development Center Inc., in collaboration with Associate Professor David A. Garvin, Harvard University Graduate School of Business Administration, and Dr. Alan Kantrow, associate editor, Harvard Business Review.

Introduction

In 1948, Colonel Radclyffe, representing the British military government in Germany, offered the Volkswagen (VW) factory as a possible buy to the Ford Motor Company. Ernest Breech, aide to Henry Ford, gave his boss this appraisal: "Mr. Ford, I don't think what we're being offered here is worth a damn."

By the end of 1949, other business leaders might have nodded in agreement. That year, total American VW unit sales were not high; the total was two.

In 1959, Doyle Dane Bernbach (DDB), a young and fairly small advertising agency in New York City, began to unroll its Volkswagen advertising campaign. The campaign consisted of a series of ads, all black and white; all in one medium, print; and all appearing in one outlet, magazines. DDB's advertising budget for that year's campaign was $800,000. By contrast, Foote, Cone & Belding spent $8 million during the Edsel's first four months. DDB's ads, however, were attention-getting, unexpected, innovative, and frank. With the advantage of hindsight, it is easy to see why they are credited with changing the face of American advertising. The ad campaign also moved product. Three years later, VW's American unit sales for the year had grown to 226,649.

The World in 1959

The VW campaign focused on one small, fuel-efficient, quite ugly, imported car. Unique as the campaign was, it was also part of an ongoing and larger story: the awkward courtship between the American public and the small-car concept. To understand that story, it is necessary to look at the postwar auto industry and the America of which it was a significant part.

The 1950s

The decade of the fifties celebrated peace, prosperity, and mobility. Shadowed by the Cold War and punctuated by the Korean conflict, the 1950s nevertheless unrolled as a time of peace and expansion. People were building families. When the soldiers returned home, the women left the assembly lines and returned home, too. The birthrate soared. Dr. Spock's book on child rearing, published in 1947, became a best-seller.

The fifties were also an era of affluence; World War II had brought an end to the Depression. The economy was expanding; over the next decade, production would double. Advertising, growing into a powerful force and helping to ensure that consumption kept pace with production, touted refrigerators, washing machines, vacuum cleaners, food mixers, pop-up toasters, the new wonder of television, and, of course, cars. Sloan Wilson, author of *The Man in the Gray Flannel Suit*, said in another of his books, "The war left [the veterans] with a lust for security and permanence, even luxury and prestige."

Permanence did not necessarily mean people were staying in one place or they were returning to their hometowns to live. With more money, people wanted new neighborhoods and new houses. Levittowns, self-contained communities that were home to populations of upward of 100,000, received the most headlines, but everywhere ranch-style and split-level houses were springing up outside the cities, accessible by new networks of highways and expressways. The number of two-car families doubled. These twin themes of togetherness and mobility were neatly captured by a car ad showing a family cooking hamburgers on a grill in front of two cars in a double carport, the caption reading, "Going our separate ways, we've never been so close."

Television, as it caught on, gave people more in common, adding to the sense of conformity that critics thought increased with the years. The quiz show "The $64,000 Question" gave Americans a chance to win more material goods. "I Love Lucy" was the top-rated program from 1952 to 1957. And disc jockey Dick Clark was there to broadcast the song "Rock around the Clock" by Bill Haley and the Comets, which, along with the songs of Chuck Berry, Buddy Holly, Little Richard, and Elvis Presley, heralded a musical revolution as well as a shift to a greater emphasis on youth.

The Auto Industry

In 1946, there were nine active producers of passenger cars in the United States: the Big Three (General Motors Corporation, Ford Motor Company, and Chrysler Corporation), Studebaker, Packard, Nash, Hudson, Kaiser-Frazer, and Crosley. There was a large backlog of demand for cars, and repeated strikes soon frustrated the producers' goal of prompt delivery. Still, consumers were buying cars and interest in automobiles remained high.

With the Korean War came a jolt. In 1950, price and production controls were imposed, regulating the prices manufacturers could charge and the quantity they could produce. Despite the war economy, consumers continued to buy cars. In 1951, sales reached 5 million, the second highest level in history. The year 1953 saw a new administration in Washington, the lifting of production controls, and the end of the war that was never officially a war. Car output expanded rapidly at the same time as the post-Korean recession emerged. The result was a reversal of the 1946 picture: Now the auto industry, characterized by a fierce selling posture, was a buyer's market. As sales fell and losses mounted, mergers reduced the number of auto producers.

The economy soon recovered. The auto industry experienced a boom year in 1955: changing styles in design, growing incomes, and looser credit terms led to retail sales of more than 7 million new cars. Many medium-priced cars were sold (see Exhibit 2.1). By the mid-1950s, small cars were on the roads as well. After the war, Crosley had offered a small model, the Bantam, although it had not sold well enough to save the company from merger. GIs returning from Germany with a taste for "mechanical oddities" had brought home a few of the VWs manufactured in Wolfsburg. By the middle of the decade, many kinds of small imported cars were reaching America—Renaults, Morris Minors, Hillman Minxes, MGs, Jaguars, and VWs—and in increasing numbers. By 1958, small foreign cars represented 8.1 percent of the U. S. market (see Exhibit 2.2).

Most of these foreign cars were not like the Volkswagen. Although small, they were also sporty, fast, and, in several cases, extremely expensive. The image of the person who drove a foreign sports car was that of a wealthy, debonair, fast-living playboy. DDB would later play on this image to sell VW's sporty Karmann Ghia in an ad that said, "Somewhere in our picture is what appears to be just another Italian playboy sitting in his expensive Italian sports car." (Additional information on new car buyers appears in Exhibit 2.3.)

The Evolution of the Small Car

While this large-scale foreign invasion of small-wheelbase cars was going on, what was Detroit doing about small cars? The Bantam, Crosley's small car, was never a big success. In its best year, 1948, only

Exhibit 2.1   Median Income of New Car Buyers by Make of Car, March 1954[a]

Low-price			Median Income[b]	
Willys	$5,808	1954		$ 4,167
Plymouth	5,837			
Chevrolet	6,308	1982		23,433
Ford	6,538			
Middle-level				
Studebaker	6,752		*Average Auto Price[c]*	
Dodge	6,766	1959		$ 2,710
Kaiser	6,883			
Nash	7,080	1983		10,725
Hudson	7,194			
Mercury	7,969			
Buick	8,438			
DeSoto	8,442			
Oldsmobile	9,063			
Chrysler	9,977			
Luxury				
Packard	10,707			
Lincoln	17,738			
Cadillac	23,306			

Median income for all new car buyers: $7,528

[a]*U.S. News and World Report*, "The People Buying New Automobiles Today," June 1955, in L.J. White, *The Auto Industry Since '45* (Cambridge, Mass.: Harvard University Press, 1971), 11.

[b]*Handbook of Labor Statistics* (Washington, D.C.: Bureau of Labor Statistics, U.S. Department of Labor, 1982).

[c]National Automobile Dealers Association.

Exhibit 2.2   Imported Car Sales

Year	Unit Sales	Percentage of U.S. Market
1955	58,000	
1957	207,000	3.5%
1958	379,000	8.1%
1959	610,000	10.2%
1980	2,174,000	24.3%
1981	2,152,000	25.2%
1982	2,083,000	26.1%
1983	2,248,000	24.4%

Source: 1955–59, adapted from L.J. White, *The Auto Industry Since '45*, (Cambridge, Mass.: Harvard University Press, 1971), 185. 1980–83, adapted from Motor Vehicle Manufacturers Association, *Motor Vehicle Facts and Figures '84*, 15.

Exhibit 2.3   Income, Age, and Occupation of New Car Buyers, 1962

	Percentage of Buyers
Annual Household Income	
Under $5,000	18.1
$5,000–$9,990	52.6
$10,000 and over	29.3
Median $6,982	100.0%
Age of Head of Household	
Under 25	2.7
25–34	22.7
35–44	28.3
45–54	23.4
55 and over	22.9
Median 43.7 years	100.0%
Occupation of Head of Household	
Professional, semiprofessional	16.5
Managers, proprietors, officials	21.4
Craftsmen, foremen	19.7
Clerical, sales	12.7
Operatives, laborers	10.8
Service workers	2.2
Farmers, farm laborers	7.5
Not employed (housewives, students, retired, and unemployed)	9.2
	100.0%

Source: Adapted from Motor Vehicle Manufacturers Association, *Auto Facts & Figures*, 1962.

25,400 units were sold. By the middle 1950s, American auto manufacturers were thinking about smaller cars, but still at a leisurely pace.
They had been fooled by an apparent small-car boom ten years earlier
and were not eager to repeat their mistakes. Some smaller cars were
on the drawing boards. By 1955, Ford had begun its plans for the
Edsel, to be ready for the market by the fall of 1957. By 1959, the Big
Three finally brought out their own compacts, if reluctantly. These
sold well and temporarily turned back the tide of small imports. Even
so, VW sales grew.

But the automakers were reluctant to take up the cause of small
cars for two major reasons. First, the Big Three tended to operate
according to a tacit agreement that had worked well in the past: What
was good for one was good for all. Edward M. Cole, head of the Chev-
rolet division, stated that the small-car market would have to reach
500,000 units before General Motors would be interested in entering
it. As one spokesman said in 1957, "If GM has said it once, it's said
it ten thousand times, a good used car is the answer to the public's
need for cheap transportation."

With hindsight, observers find it easy to criticize Detroit for
shortsighted self-interest. The Big Three did fear that open announce-

ment of next year's small car would cut into sales of this year's big car. But Detroit also believed it was taking signals from the public. These signals suggested Americans preferred a small car that was a little bigger, a simple car that was a little fancier. Detroit's ads at the time tended to play down economy and efficiency and play up grandeur.

Accordingly, as soon as Detroit introduced compacts, these smaller cars began to grow. They grew in size and in cost. From 1961 to 1968, a low-priced Detroit compact would add 2 inches to its wheelbase, 4 to 5 inches to its length, and $300 to its price. When Detroit introduced the basic no-frills compact and offered for a premium deluxe interior and exterior trim, 60 to 70 percent of the buyers ordered the deluxe model.

Meanwhile, VW was becoming a more visible presence. In the middle 1950s, it took two steps that substantially increased sales. First, it set up a wholly owned subsidiary, Volkswagen of America (VOA), that included 1,000 franchised dealers. Other foreign-car producers had relied on novelty to sell their cars; they had not bothered to build a solid dealer and service and repair system. Some, like Renault, had seen sales fall drastically as a result. VW, by contrast, built a system that put service before sales and provided a solid dealer system to offer that service.

Second, VOA hired DDB.

"Think Small"

DDB designed an ad campaign that was as unconventional as the car it was trying to sell. As Al Steiner, currently VOA account executive for DDB (and a man who has been on the account since 1961), commented, "How would you have sold an ugly car with the engine in the wrong end?"

It is hard to remember now how preposterous those first VWs seemed. To many first viewers the car resembled an insect—a bug, beetle, or slug.

On the other hand, it ran on about half the fuel needed to run Detroit's cars, and its tires lasted longer. Since the model barely changed from year to year, supplying parts through the dealerships was easy. It wasn't a beautiful car. It did have a refreshing simplicity, and it was a sound car. Recalled Steiner:

One thing that preceded the advertising was a trip to Germany that Doyle and Bernbach took, along with Helmut Krone and Julian Koenig—the people who worked on the account first. What rubbed off was a kind of Volkswageny attitude. It seemed absurd to us at first that so much time was spent on inspectors and inspecting. It was fascinating to find that the chief inspector reported to the president of the company rather than to the production manager. There are things you can deduce about a company that is run that way.

To promote this car, DDB designed a campaign that was, in agency executives' words, "direct, honest . . . with a bright, irreverent tone." Each ad featured one large photo of a car (photos were uncommon in auto ads in 1959), a headline that was both a caption and a lead for the copy (and always ended with a period), and copy that ran from 159 words to 976 (so that it ran on even less gas than the car itself).

Some sample headlines:

- Ugly is only skin-deep.
- Mr. Kennedy and his 1947, 1955, 1956, 1958, 1961, 1962, 1963, 1965 Volkswagen.
- They said it couldn't be done. It couldn't.
- It takes this many men to inspect this many Volkswagens.
- What if it poops out in Paducah?
- Some shapes are hard to improve on.

The ads are shown in Exhibits 2.4–2.8.

The World in 1984

Twenty-five years after it began the campaign, DDB still held the VW account. The New York-based firm had a branch office in Troy, Michigan, across the street from VOA national headquarters. The campaign still received awards.

The automotive world had changed, however. Skyrocketing fuel costs had led to a rising demand for small, fuel-efficient cars. By 1980, Japan had become the world's top producer of motor vehicles. Imported cars had reached nearly 27 per cent of total car sales, with Japanese cars (Hondas, Subarus, Toyotas, Mazdas, Datsuns) accounting for four-fifths of the total. In 1980, one out of every five cars sold in America was Japanese. An increase in U. S. small-car production capacity and the establishment, in 1981, of a voluntary export restraint program that limited Japanese exports of cars to the United States caused a decline in Japanese car sales. Moreover, some Japanese cars were being produced in the United States, and others were being planned. Toyota, for example, had recently agreed to a joint venture with General Motors. Overall, the small-car share of total auto sales stood at about 60 percent. The total number of cars sold in 1984 was about 10.6 million.

In 25 years, America had also seen significant social changes. There had been a shift to a more conservative climate, brought on partly by the economic realities of the late 1970s; the population was aging; buyers were concerned with material things and with quality. They tended to buy less often and to buy better quality when they did. And the market was more segmented. The number of working

Exhibit 2.4

Source: Courtesy of Volkswagen of America.

Exhibit 2.5

Source: Courtesy of Volkswagen of America.

Exhibit 2.6

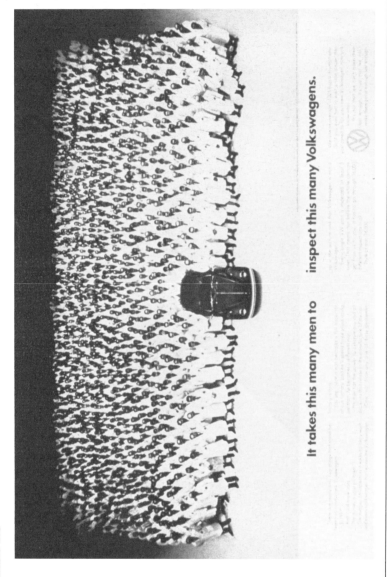

Source: Courtesy of Volkswagen of America.

Exhibit 2.7

What if it poops out in Paducah?

Source: Courtesy of Volkswagen of America.

women had risen from 21 million to 43 million. Exhibit 2.9 shows how these changes altered the profile of the typical auto buyer.

Summarizing these changes, Al Steiner observed:

We are talking to a market that will spend, on average, $11,000 for their automobile; a market that will, on average, take almost four years to pay for them; and a market, on average, that plans to keep

Exhibit 2.8

Some shapes are hard to improve on.

Ask any hen.

You just can't design a more functional shape for an egg.

And we figure the same is true of the Volkswagen Sedan.

Don't think we haven't tried. (As a matter of fact, the VW's been changed nearly 3,000 times.)

But we can't improve our basic design.

Like the egg, it's the right kind of package for what goes inside.

So that's where most of our energy goes.

To get more power without using more gas. To put synchromesh on first gear. To improve the heater. That kind of thing.

As a result, our package carries four adults, and their luggage, at about 32 miles to a gallon of regular gas and 40,000 miles to a set of tires.

We've made a few external changes, of course. Such as push-button doorknobs.

Which is one up on the egg.

Dealer Name

Source: Courtesy of Volkswagen of America.

their new cars for at least five years. Obviously, they don't want to make a mistake.

Exhibit 2.9   Most New-Car Finance Terms Made for Four-Year Mark

CHARACTERISTICS OF AUTOMOBILE OWNERS AND DRIVERS

Characteristic	Domestic Cars		Imported Cars	
	Registered Owner	Principal Driver	Registered Owner	Principal Driver
Sex				
Male	70.4%	56.6%	64.6%	53.4%
Female	29.6	43.4	35.4	46.6
Total	100.0%	100.0%	100.0%	100.0%
Age				
Under 18	0.1%	0.4%	0.2%	0.5%
18–24	6.8	8.1	11.3	12.5
25–29	9.8	10.3	19.2	20.2
30–34	9.4	9.6	18.0	17.9
35–39	11.0	10.8	15.6	15.1
40–44	8.6	8.3	8.6	8.4
45–49	7.2	7.1	5.8	5.2
50–54	9.9	9.5	5.7	5.8
55–64	18.4	17.6	9.9	9.1
65 and over	18.7	18.3	5.7	5.5
Median Age	48.0	46.7	35.4	34.7
Employment				
Administrative/management ...	21.7%	17.2%	29.0%	24.1%
Professional/technical	22.3	21.6	34.2	36.1
Craftspeople/laborers	18.7	16.2	11.2	11.6
Office/clerical	6.9	10.2	6.4	7.5
Sales personnel	5.0	5.3	7.2	6.4
Student	0.7	1.3	1.4	2.1
Retired	21.6	20.6	7.0	6.3
Homemaker	2.3	6.8	2.6	4.7
Other	1.0	0.9	0.9	1.1
Total	100.0%	100.0%	100.0%	100.0%
Personal Income				
Under $10,000	9.5%	15.9%	8.6%	12.5%
$10,000–$14,999	13.0	15.3	11.7	15.2
$15,000–$19,999	13.9	14.6	13.3	14.0
$20,000–$24,999	15.7	15.2	15.6	15.7
$25,000–$34,999	21.8	18.3	22.5	19.5
$35,000–$49,999	14.3	11.4	12.2	10.2
$50,000–$74,999	6.9	5.2	8.7	7.4
$75,000 and Over	5.0	4.2	7.4	5.4
Total	100.0%	100.0%	100.0%	100.0%
Median (000)	$ 24.3	$ 21.4	$ 25.3	$ 22.6

Note: The above data are from a study of a sample of buyers of new domestic and imported automobiles registered during January and February, 1983.

Source: *Buyers of New Domestic Cars*, 1983 and *Buyers of New Imported Cars*, 1983. Copyright 1983. *Newsweek, Inc.* Reproduced with permission.

Exhibit 2.9 *continued*

NEW-CAR PURCHASE CHARACTERISTICS

Characteristic	Domestic	Import
Replaced Previous Car		
Did	85.0%	76.5%
Did Not	15.0	23.5
Total	100.0%	100.0%
Year Model Cars Replaced		
1983	0.3%	0.5%
1982	6.0	4.7
1981	10.3	8.0
1980	14.9	14.1
1979	13.8	12.1
1978	12.7	12.6
1977	10.6	11.0
1976	10.6	9.8
1975	4.2	6.9
1974	4.3	6.9
Pre 1974	13.8	15.6
Total	101.5%[a]	102.2%[a]
Financing		
Did Finance	69.3%	76.0%
Did Not Finance	30.7	24.0
Total	100.0%	100.0%
Length of Finance Contract		
Less than 12 Months	2.0%	1.7%
12–23 Months	2.6	2.2
24–35 Months	6.6	6.1
36–47 Months	19.9	25.6
48–59 Months	67.6	59.1
60 Months or more	1.3	5.3
Total	100.0%	100.0%
Principal Usage		
To and From Work	42.6%	54.8%
Pleasure Trips	15.8	9.5
Local Transportation	32.2	22.6
Business	8.3	11.2
School	1.0	1.6
Other	0.2	0.3
Total	100.0%	100.0%

Exhibit 2.9   *continued*

Characteristic	Domestic	Import
Plan to Keep Car		
One Year	3.9%	2.2%
Two Years	10.5	6.6
Three Years	17.6	13.5
Four Years	18.3	13.4
Five Years	23.1	26.0
Six Years	7.4	8.0
Seven Years	3.2	4.7
Eight Years	3.3	4.1
Nine Years	0.4	0.2
Ten or More Years	12.4	21.4
Total	100.0%	100.0%
Median Years	5.0	5.5

ªIncludes multiple mentions.

Note: The above data are from a study of a sample of buyers of new domestic and imported automobiles registered during January and February, 1983.

Source: *Buyers of New Domestic Cars*, 1983 and *Buyers of New Imported Cars*, 1983. Copyright 1983. *Newsweek, Inc.* Reproduced with permission.

Sources

Automobile Facts & Figures. Detroit: Motor Vehicles Manufacturers Association. Yearly.

Buyers of New Domestic Cars, 1983. New York: Newsweek Inc., 1983.

Buyers of New Imported Cars, 1983. New York: Newsweek Inc., 1983.

Chang, C. S. *The Japanese Auto Industry and the U. S. Market*. New York: Praeger Publishers, 1981.

Doyle Dane Bernbach. "The Story of Volkswagen." Script.

Handbook of Labor Statistics. Washington, D. C.: Bureau of Labor Statistics, U. S. Department of Labor, 1982.

Lewis, P. *The Fifties*. New York: J. B. Lippincott Co., 1978.

National Automobile Dealers Association, McLean, VA.

Rowsome Jr., F. *Think Small: The Story of Those Volkswagen Ads*. Brattleboro, VT.: The Stephen Greene Press, 1970.

U. S. Industrial Outlook: Prospects for Over 300 Industries. 25th annual edition. Washington, D. C.: U. S. Department of Commerce/Bureau of Industrial Economics, January 1984.

VW sales figures, 1949–1981, (correspondence).

White, L. J., *The Auto Industry Since '45*. Cambridge, MA.: Harvard University Press, 1971.

Case 3

Milano Sportswear

Developed by Professor Kristina Cannon-Bonventre, Northeastern University College of Business Administration, in collaboration with Professor David A. Garvin, Harvard University Graduate School of Business Administration.

Luca Adagio, president of Milano Sportswear and a noted Italian designer, was in a quandary.

Our biggest decision this year, and perhaps in the firm's history, needs to be made this afternoon. We've been collecting data, mulling over all the information, discussing, discussing, discussing. As usual, the data don't speak for themselves. We're going to have to face the music this afternoon and decide—should we broaden the distribution of our high fashion, exclusive sweater line?

The sweaters, although machine made, appeared to be one of a kind. They were big sellers in Adagio's small boutiques in the fashion districts of Milan, Rome, Paris, Madrid, and London. In 1980, Adagio had introduced the sweaters to the United States where they were sold in a small number of upscale boutiques and a few select department stores such as Bergdorf Goodman and Neiman-Marcus. The sweaters, priced at about $300, were as successful in the United States as they had been in Europe.

For more than two years, other specialty stores, department stores, catalogs, and off-price retailers had been asking Adagio to sell to them. Since the firm's profit as a percentage of revenues had been declining for two years, Adagio thought that perhaps Milano should consider broadening distribution away from strictly exclusive retailers.

Exhibit 3.1   Operating Results (Percentage of Sales)

	1980	1981	1982	1983	1984	1985	Compound Annual Growth Rate
Net Sales	100%	100%	100%	100%	100%	100%	23.4%
Cost of Sales	45	47	49	51	50	51	
Gross Margin	55	53	51	49	50	49	20.6
Expenses	30	33	34	35	37	38	29.4
Payroll	14.0	15.0	16.0	16.5	16.5	16.0	26.7
Rent	2.5	4.0	5.0	5.5	7.5	8.5	57.6
Advertising	7.0	7.0	6.0	5.5	5.0	5.0	15.4
General & Admin.	5.0	5.0	5.0	5.0	5.0	5.0	23.4
Theft	0.5	1.0	1.0	1.5	1.5	2.5	70.3
Overhead	0.5	0.5	0.5	0.5	0.5	0.5	23.4
Other	0.5	0.5	0.5	0.5	1.0	0.5	23.4
Operating Income	25.0	20.0	17.0	14.0	13.0	11.0	4.7
Taxes							
Net Income							

History of Milano Sportswear

After making his name as a designer in the high-fashion world in the 1950s and 1960s, Luca Adagio had the idea of opening a small number of boutiques in major European cities. His boutiques sold a small line of very fashionable and high-priced sportswear designed for women to wear at resorts, on yachts, and so on. Each boutique was small, uncluttered, and quietly elegant. Soft classical and popular music provided a background for shopping. Most of the sweater designs were shown on elegant mannequins, and no sweaters were hung on racks, to avoid stretching. Clients requested their size, and sweaters were brought out from the back room. On busy shopping days, models wore the sweaters while they assisted the regular clerks. The sportswear line became a status symbol among wealthy, fashionable women, many of whom had originally been customers for Adagio's high-fashion gowns and other elegant clothing. He numbered movie stars and royalty among his clients. Operating results for Milano Sportswear are presented in Exhibit 3.1. A print advertisement for typical sweater designs is presented in Exhibit 3.2.

In the fashion business, it was always difficult to understand why clients found particular lines appealing, why some lines continued to be popular, and which lines would be successful in future seasons.

*This business is positively crazy! Just when you think you have a handle on your clients' tastes, something or someone comes along and upsets the whole thing. Our sweaters have (knock wood) developed into a bit of a classic–they're beautiful, wearable, and not **too** available.*

—Adagio's marketing assistant

Luca's sweaters are always "right." If we change our plans sud-

Exhibit 3.2   Milano Sportswear Print Advertisement

denly on holiday, I know that my stock of sweaters means that I've still packed the right things. My friends and I even enjoy competing to have Luca's latest designs first.

—A frequent client

Luca's sweaters are one of my best fashion finds. I love to wear them and be seen in them. I also never worry that I'll end up seeing everyone wearing the same sweater.

—A happy client

Since we started offering Milano sweaters we've developed a whole set of affluent, new, frequent customers. The sweaters have such appeal, and they are different from other stores in our area. Most of our sweater customers don't walk out with just a sweater purchase. That shopping

trip leads to trousers, skirts, shoes, accessories—the works.
> —Buyer, U. S. upscale
> department store

*I've often thought about just **why** the sweaters have been successful. After all, they aren't the **only** sweaters in the world! I believe— I can't really say, I **know**—that it's for three primary reasons. They're always in rich, jewel-like colors such as sapphire blue, ruby red, emerald green; the fit is at once flattering to most figures and very feminine; and they're suitable for a wide range of social occasions.*
> —Marketing director,
> Milano Sportswear

Recent Developments

A number of recent developments had prompted Adagio to listen more seriously to other retailers that wanted to sell his sweaters. He had the manufacturing capacity to produce more sweaters. He had also discovered that designing the sweaters, from color choices to overall shape to producing a few innovative features each season, was something he enjoyed. And, as the number of *haute couture* clients in his and other firms declined, he found he had the time and energy to do it.

Competition for the high end of the business had recently intensified. This was the result of other designers shifting more of their efforts to undertakings similar to Milano Sportswear, the increasing numbers of newly successful Japanese and American designers, and the attempts of a number of American clothing manufacturers to attract the more wealthy female customers by dramatically upgrading their lines. The increase in competition, combined with only modest increases in the number of customers similar to the present clientele, limited the possibilities for significant growth in the near future.

Some of the cost of doing business had increased faster than net sales (see Exhibit 3.1). This, in turn, meant the profitability was declining. Rents, for example, in the high-fashion districts of major cities were continuing to climb, and the competition for prime space put landlords in a strong bargaining position. And since Milano's loyal and experienced employees were valuable assets to the firm, Adagio believed they could not be asked to forgo pay increases. Many, in fact, might be forced to look elsewhere, and Adagio thought his competitors would benefit from their availability.

Last, the existing stores and locations had probably saturated their local markets. Even though clients were wealthy, they were not turning over their entire sportswear wardrobes annually. Adagio's sweaters had a classic elegance that kept their owners wearing them for several years.

In this market, Adagio was facing pressures from the competition as well as from the behavior of consumers. He was prepared to look carefully at the retail alternatives and also to look at other ways to reverse the decline in profitability in the existing outlets. He and his associates had discussed various possibilities, including reducing expenses, adding men's sweaters, adding children's sweaters, and introducing a line of clothing items other than sweaters.

The Controversy

In the previous several months, Adagio had talked with people inside and outside the firm about adding new retailers to the distribution of the sweater line. Because the Milano employees were a close-knit group, Adagio brought them in on major decisions early in the process. Milano also had close relationships with the current retailers, because there were few and buyers tended to know each other personally. And, because many of the clients were longtime customers who also had clothes custom made, they tended to hear the gossip in the workrooms and made comments during fittings. The idea of broadening the distribution of the sweaters tended to evoke strong feelings:

It's a splendid idea. We need somehow to broaden our customer base and revenue possibilities if we're going to grow the way we need to. We're too dependent on a narrow line that is too subject to the ups and downs of fashion.

—Chief financial officer,
Milano Sportswear

This decision scares me for at least two reasons. I'm not sure that we have the people to carry this out. Sure, we can makes lots of beautiful sweaters, but what about keeping up the relationships with all those added retailers and the services they will expect? What happens when several stores in one city start battling it out for customers and end up marking down all our sweaters? What kind of prices will they demand from us next year, and the year after?

—Head of marketing operations,
Milano Sportswear

I can't believe Luca would do this to me! Pierre Cardin, Ralph Lauren, Halston—they all sold out. I thought that I could trust Luca to maintain his integrity.

—Longtime haute couture and
sportswear client

What nerve! We helped Luca get his start in the U. S. We've featured his sweaters in our designer boutiques, and we've all done well partly because the sweaters were something special and different from

what other stores carried. Now ... I can't promise to be so loyal.
—Buyer, U.S. upscale department store

I'm positively ecstatic! I've been begging Luca to please, please, please let us handle his sweaters. Maybe it's about to happen.
—Buyer, U.S. department store
(not currently a Milano client)

Before we start selling our wonderful sweaters to every Tom, Dick, and Harry in retailing, why don't we look at other opportunities? What about men's and children's apparel and things besides sweaters? I think that it's a mistake to sell to everybody.
—Design director, Milano Sportswear

We are probably talking about shifting from a push to a pull strategy if we hope to expand our volume very much. With our current push strategy, we have small amounts of advertising and we rely on the stores to push our sweaters. With pull, we would need to advertise directly to consumers so they would go into stores for our sweaters. That's a whole new ball game—more advertising to consumers, more expensive advertising. My job and the staff that I would need would change dramatically.
—Director of advertising and promotion,
Milano Sportswear

If we broaden our distribution to more markets, what we really need to address is the issue of product positioning. We can't ignore the relationship between the kinds of goods we produce and the kinds of stores in which they are sold.
—Marketing director, Milano Sportswear

Retail Alternatives

The alternative retail store types that Milano Sportswear might choose to carry the sweater line included department stores, specialty store chains, catalog retailers, and off-price chains. Selected illustrations of store interiors are presented in Exhibit 3.3.

Department Stores

Department stores had the largest physical space, averaging 200,000 square feet. They also had the largest amount and variety of goods offered and in the most widely varying price ranges. Although department stores varied widely from store to store, from one city to another, and from one chain to another, they all served a very broad customer base. Located in central business districts and in suburban

Exhibit 3.3   Illustrations of Some Retail Store Types

Source: Courtesy of Zayre Corporation.

malls, department stores typically carried apparel; home accessories such as linens, china, and crystal; and various gift items. Many also carried such hard goods as home appliances, furniture, and photographic equipment. Because of their size and their quantity of merchandise, department stores had traditionally defined their target customers as the entire middle and upper class in their geographic areas.

Many traditional department stores were facing competition from off-price retailers, from upscale stores that were expanding geographically, and from specialty stores. In recent years, many department stores had sharply reduced store services to reduce operating costs. Frequently, the only contact a shopper had with store personnel was at the cash register. Many stores were making heavy use of newspapers, fliers, and coupons to advertise price promotions, in an attempt to move merchandise more quickly. Observers believed that many consumers had developed a pattern of waiting for promotions before buying. By the mid-1980s, many department stores were remodeling old buildings rather than building new stores. The remodeling included creating more attractive backgrounds for merchandise, designer boutiques, stores within a store based on such themes as "The French Country Collection," lifestyle shops offering a full selection of items in one place, and fashionable restaurants or other store services. By remodeling, stores hoped to create exciting shopping environments to attract new customers and retain existing ones.

Specialty Stores

Specialty stores were smaller stores specializing in serving a specific target market with a particular category of goods and offering higher service levels than traditional department stores. Many were parts of larger chains. Casual Corner, for example, was a 585-store chain in 42 states offering a mix of dress and career fashions and casual ready-to-wear and sportswear. The merchandise was of medium to better quality and emphasized updated classic styles. The stores averaged 4,500 square feet and emphasized an open, comfortable shopping atmosphere. The stores catered to younger women, typically under 35.

August Max, with 32 stores, offered contemporary fashions of better quality. It tended to be somewhat more fashion forward than Casual Corner. The average store had 3,500 square feet, had an elegant atmosphere, and was located in a shopping mall that attracted affluent clientele.

The Shop for Pappagallo consisted of more than 200 retail shops offering Pappagallo footwear, accessories, and clothing in home-like surroundings. They were located in the more expensive malls and within some large department stores. The target market consisted of younger women, and the offerings included both casual and career wear.

Each of these specialty shop chains emphasized a pleasant and attractive shopping environment enhanced by personal service. Specialty stores such as these had grown rapidly and were continuing to grow.

Off-Price Retailers

Off-price retailers had become a major force in American retailing during the preceding decade. They varied widely in size and type, from small specialty shops such as Hit or Miss, with 400 shops catering to fashionable career women, to department stores such as Filene's Basement and T. J. Maxx, which offered men's, women's, and children's clothing, and home furnishings. Off-price retailers' lines were frequently incomplete, because they often purchased leftovers from orders or goods that did not sell in regular stores and some irregulars and seconds. They had become enormously popular and were a source of outstanding fashion and staple values year after year. Shopping in Filene's Basement, for example, had become so popular for Boston residents and tourists that by the 1980s the Basement had opened freestanding stores in suburban malls.

T. J. Maxx, with 156 apparel "supermarts," was the second largest store of this type in the United States. By 1984, the chain was undertaking a large updating to project a more upbeat, contemporary look. All the off-price retailers used a self-service approach, and most concentrated on excellent store layout and signs to facilitate easy shopping. Off-price stores had attracted many middle- and upper-income shoppers.

Retail Catalogs

Retail catalogs had also grown rapidly in the preceding decade. Their success was attributed, to a great extent, to career women falling short of time for shopping. It was also the result of declines in in-store service levels among department stores. Many consumers had come to the conclusion that the time, energy, and cost of driving to and shopping at suburban malls was frequently not worth the effort. The successful catalogs such as The Talbots and Jos. A. Banks catered to career-minded, affluent men and women with updated classic clothing. They offered a range of clothing and accessories for office, dress, and casual occasions. Both Jos. A. Banks and The Talbots also had retail stores: 19 stores and 39 stores, respectively. Exhibit 3.4 presents a typical catalog cover.

Making the Decision

Adagio believed he needed to consider five categories of information before deciding:

Exhibit 3.4   Typical Catalog Cover

FALL/HOLIDAY 1985

Source: Courtesy of The Talbots.

- The potential customer.
- The financial implications of moving to a higher volume business.
- The effects on the image of the sweater line and on Milano Sportswear.
- The response of Milano's current retailers to broadening the distribution of the sweaters.
- The alternatives to broadened distribution, such as cost cutting or offering other lines to current retail customers.

The Potential Customer

The potential customer for Milano sweaters, as currently priced, included both women who were buying the sweater for their own use and women or men purchasing the sweater as a gift. In addition to more mature, affluent women with large clothing budgets, the potential customers might include younger women living at home who were able to spend most of their incomes on themselves as well as career women who bought expensive clothing to enhance their images.

The price of the sweaters led most of the Milano Sportswear staff to think of the purchase as planned. However, in any store the customer would be presented with a wide range of competing products. Therefore, some buyers would have gone shopping specifically for a Milano sweater and others might have ended up with one after setting out to shop more generally. Predicting the behavior of consumers shopping for fashion items was known to be difficult.

The Financial Implications

The financial implications of moving from a low-volume, high-margin business to a higher volume business were also difficult to predict. Could Milano broaden its customer base and still expect that the sweaters could be priced as high? In trying to reach more customers, would more advertising and promotion expenses be incurred? Would any of the large retailers demand special prices from Milano, thus putting pressure on Milano's margins? Adagio had heard from colleagues that similar shifts by competitors had led to average margin declines of 20 to 30 percent. Would broadening distribution dilute the Milano image, thus weakening the retailers' ability to command full price? For calculating these impacts, Milano's financial staff had developed a financial work sheet similar to the one in Exhibit 3.5.

The Image

The image of the sweater line and of Milano Sportswear was currently high fashion and high priced. Supplying only Milano's boutiques and a few other selected shops and department stores had contributed to

Exhibit 3.5   Financial Work Sheet (1985 estimates)

	Milano Boutique (5 stores)	Other Current U.S. Retailers (10 locations)	Specialty Store	Department Store	Off-Price Retailer	Catalog
Retail selling price/sweater (average)[1]	$300	$300				
Avg. number of sweaters sold/ week/store[2]	75	35	10–15	15–20	15–25	15–30
Total sweater sales/store (annual, $000s)[3]	$1,170	$546				
Manufacturer's cost of goods sold/sweater[4]	$73.50	$73.50				
Retailer's cost of goods sold/ sweater[5]	$150	$150				
Manufacturer's gross margin/ sweater[6]	$76.50	$76.50				
Manufacturer's expenses/sweater[7]	$57	$57				
Manufacturer's operating income/ sweater[8]	$16.50	$16.50				
Retailer's gross margin/ sweater[9]	$150	$150				

[1]Retail selling price: For existing retailers, this is given in the case, page 1.

[2]Average number of sweaters sold per store per week: Data in first two columns are for current retailers and are, therefore, accurate; data in columns three through six are estimates prepared by Milano staff.

[3]Total dollar sweater sales/store (annual $000s): Retail price per sweater × number of sweaters sold per week × 52.

[4]Manufacturer's cost of goods sold (per sweater): Regular price retailers typically double their cost from the manufacturer. Therefore, the retailer paid $150 per sweater. This $150 is both the manufacturer's selling price and the retailer's cost of goods sold.

In order to calculate the manufacturer's cost of goods sold, we work backwards. In Exhibit 1, the current manufacturer's cost of sales or cost of goods sold is 51 percent of net sales or the manufacturer's selling price. Therefore: .51 × $150 = $76.50 = manufacturer's cost of goods sold.

[5]Retailer's cost of goods sold: This is $150 (see note 4).

[6]Manufacturer's gross margin: This is the manufacturer's selling price minus manufacturer's cost of goods sold, or $150 − 76.50 = $73.50 (see note 4).

[7]Manufacturer's expenses per sweater: Exhibit 1 gives this currently as 38 percent of net sales or of the manufacturer's selling price: .38 × $150 = $57.

[8]Manufacturer's operating income per sweater: Exhibit 1 gives this currently as 11 percent of net sales at the manufacturer's selling price:

.11 × $150 = $16.50.

Operating income is also: $73.50 − $57 = $16.50.

[9]Retailer's gross margin per sweater: Retailer's selling price minus retailer's cost of goods sold: $300 − $150 = $150 (see notes 1, 5, 6).

that image. How much could Milano broaden distribution and keep the special position held by the sweaters? Which of the retailers among the various options would contribute to the image? Since Milano would not be able to control exactly how the sweaters were presented in the retail settings, the company had to place great trust in any retailers it supplied.

What Response Might Milano Expect from Current Retailers?

Would current retailers be willing to feature Milano sweaters if other stores nearby also had them? Would current retailers retaliate by canceling or reducing orders? When Halston agreed to design for J. C. Penney Company, for example, Bergdorf Goodman, accounting for 10 percent of his ready-to-wear line, canceled all his orders. Others subsequently followed suit. Would Milano suffer a similar fate? Or could such problems be prevented?

Adagio left his office for the meeting. He was nervous and excited. They could make it work, but how?

Case 4

Gelateria Italia*

Developed by Professor Michael J. Roberts, Harvard University Graduate School of Business Administration, in collaboration with Professor David A. Garvin, Harvard University Graduate School of Business Administration.

GELATERIA ITALIA (A)

Well, said Paula, this is it. We've been studying the situation long enough. We need to decide whether we are serious about going ahead with this business or not. We can't afford to waste any more time. Let's crunch through the numbers, get together Saturday morning, and make a decision.

With that, the three students headed home for the evening, wondering what the Saturday morning—three days from now—would bring.

Overview

Paula Wilson, Eric Rogers, and Mark Rodman were in their final year at Great Plains College, a small four-year college in Carlton, Indiana. The students had worked together on several projects during their senior year, cementing the friendship that had formed during their freshman year.

As the spring semester—their last—began, the three had begun

---

*Note: The Gelateria Italia case series consists of two cases—Gelateria Italia (A) and Gelateria Italia (B). The (A) case is intended for use with the (B) case, although the (A) case can be used on a stand-alone basis. Readings follow each case and provide an explanation of some of the material covered in the case. These readings will prove very helpful in preparing the cases.

sharing their career plans and realized that each of them had, at one time or another, thought about running their own business. The focus of their discussion turned to "How do we get there?" Paula, Mark, and Eric brought up two possible routes for achieving their goal:

1.   They could go to work for a few years

    ▪   Each could pick a particular business, like retail sales, printing, and so on, and really try to learn the business, and then start a company.
    ▪   They could opt to work for a bank and learn financial skills, make some contacts, and try to buy a business in a few years.

2.   They could try something right now. It would be easier when they were younger; they'd have fewer commitments and could put in more hours.

Over a few beers one night, Paula, Mark, and Eric decided a business of their own was worth a try—after all, what did they really have to lose?

The Search

The three began talking with their professors at school, trying to determine what would be a good way for them to get into business. Many of their professors counseled them to wait until they had some more management experience, but they had already decided to give it a try *now*. One professor suggested they talk with the trust and estate departments of the local banks. He said that if someone who owned a business died, these departments would have to sell the business to get the money for the heirs—perhaps they could buy a business in this manner.

     The three students talked about the two options they perceived—buying a business or starting one. It seemed it would probably take less money to start a business than to buy one, but they really didn't have any ideas. Paula, Mark, and Eric decided it was worth looking around for a business to buy. They were bound to learn something, and maybe they would even get lucky and stumble on to a good opportunity.

     The three made an appointment to speak with the trust officer of the local bank. Eric recalled their conversation:

     This banker just kept asking us questions about how much money we had, or what we could put up as collateral to borrow the money. He didn't spend any time trying to figure out whether we could really run a business.

     The three were discouraged and agreed that they would get together after spring break and reformulate their plan.

The Idea

Mark had visited his parents in Boston during Easter break and had stopped in to see some friends in New York on the way back to Carlton. In Boston, he had noticed one or two gelati stores and had seen eight or ten in New York. He had tasted, and enjoyed, this thicker, richer, tastier Italian version of ice cream. This was it! This was the idea around which they could build a business.

Mark came back full of enthusiasm; he shared his idea with Eric and Paula. Paula talked about why the idea was appealing:

It seemed to have the elements we were looking for; it's a business we could easily learn, and it's not that complicated to run. It's not like we're starting a computer company or something. And, let's face it, we really haven't come up with anything else.

As the three discussed the idea, a concept emerged. Gelati was the Italian equivalent of ice cream. It was made by a delicate method mixing cream, milk, sugar, and flavorings. The key to the process was to make it slowly and not to whip any air into the product. With very little air, gelati could be served at a warmer temperature than ice cream. Because it was less cold than regular ice cream, the flavors came through more clearly.

Carlton was a college town, with some light industry as well. The town had its share of bookstores, pizza parlors and pubs, and a few drugstores and snack bars sold ice cream, as well as hamburgers and sandwiches. But there was no establishment dedicated to ice cream.

Paula, Mark, and Eric thought they could create a European-style cafe, serving coffee and pastry in the morning, coffee and gelati all day, and some light sandwiches and beverages at the lunch and dinner hour. They christened their potential business *Gelateria Italia*.

As the first order of business, they needed to learn about gelati. Was it hard to make? Could they buy it somewhere? Mark called some of the stores he had seen in Boston and New York, and most of them reported making their own gelati. Mark did find two stores, however, that bought the product from a supplier outside New York. This company—Italian Specialty Products Inc. (ISP)—sold gelati to a few freestanding stores in the northeast and to several chains of department stores (i.e., Bloomingdales), which operated small units in the gourmet departments.

Mark talked with ISP, and the company was willing to sell gelati to them. ISP said the product would cost $7 per gallon, and that it could be shipped via refrigerated truck for roughly $1 a gallon. The average store was able to get about 20 servings from each gallon of gelati, ISP reported.

The students decided to spend the next couple of weeks investigating the idea. Eric would investigate the market potential and try to estimate what sales level the store could achieve; Paula would look

at real estate and equipment. She would try to determine what kind
of rental space was available, how much it would cost, and how much
the equipment would cost. Mark would try to do some financial fore-
casts and investigate where they could raise the money. They decided
to meet all day Sunday, April 20, to review their progress.

The Meeting

Eric kicked things off by discussing the market potential:

*I have spent some time at Jack's Snack Bar and Nesbitt's Drug
Store. On an average afternoon, they sell (together) 25 ice cream cones
an hour at $0.75 each; at night, they sell 40 to 50 ice creams per hour,
for a total of roughly 250 servings per day.*

*I figure we could sell a lot more ice cream since it would be the
focus of our business; also, we will charge a higher price, say $1.00 per
serving. If some people buy coffee or another snack, this will raise our
average check to say $1.50. Weekends and the summer should be even
higher, but as a first cut, we could assume 350 customers for ice cream
and beverage at an average check of $1.50. Then for breakfast, lunch,
and dinner customers, I assumed we would serve a total of 100 customers with an average check of $5.00; $4.00 for food, and $1.00 for
coffee and/or other beverage.*

*I also assumed that we would want to do some advertising and
promotion. We should assume $100 per week for ads in the school and
local papers.*

Paula talked about her investigation:

*I've been looking at real estate on Grand Street—I assumed it was
worth it to be right in the center of town, near the shopping district. I
assumed we would need 1,200 square feet of space:*

- 200 feet for storage and freezer
- 300 feet for the counter and kitchen area
- 700 feet for tables and chairs

*This prime space will cost us $12.00 per foot per year, plus another 30
percent for utilities, insurance, and contribution to the block's security
and merchant's fund.*

I also looked at equipment. I assumed we would need the following:

Tables and chairs	$ 2,000
China, glass, and silverware	1,000
Leasehold improvements:	
electricity, plumbing, tile, air-conditioning, painting, signs, and counters	60,000
Storage and counter freezers	25,000
Espresso/cappucino machines	5,000
Cash registers	2,000
TOTAL	$95,000

Mark talked about what he had learned:

I started to talk to some people about possibly investing in the company, but the first thing they wanted to see was some financial projections for the business. I thought we should put off talking seriously with anyone until we can present these. Also, we really don't know how much money we need until we do these projections. Finally, the projections will help **us** *decide whether the business is an attractive opportunity.*

I investigated several items in order to develop the following assumptions, which we will need to complete our projections:

- *Assume sales revenues as described by Eric; assume that the shop is open 360 days per year;*
- *Assume cost of product (COGS) is 40 percent for gelati and beverages and 50 percent for food items;*
- *Assume salaries as follows: Eric, Mark, and Paula, $25,000 each per year; and part-time help of four people each day for eight-hour shifts at $5.00 per hour per person including benefits;*
- *Assume rent and real estate expenses as described;*
- *Assume advertising and promotion expenses as described;*
- *Assume general and administrative expenses of $250 per week for phone, uniforms, cleaning, and so forth;*
- *Assume depreciable life of five years on all equipment and leasehold improvements. Assume 40 percent tax rate.*

In order to develop a cash flow statement, we also need to make some assumptions regarding investments in equipment and working capital:

- *Assume equipment costs as outlined by Paula;*
- *Assume we would need $5,000 in working capital to fund salaries and hourly wages, and an inventory of gelati, paper goods, etc.*

As their meeting ended, they tried to review what their objectives were. Mark outlined them as follows:

We feel that the business is going to be successful, but we have to remember that to potential investors, the main factor in their decisions is how attractive the business is as an investment. In order to make a convincing argument, we need to develop a projection of income and cash flow to present to them. Even more importantly, we need to figure out how much money we are going to need to come up with, and whether the business is an attractive venture for **us**.

With that, Paula chimed in, "Time is running out. If we decide that we are not going to go ahead with this, we better do it quickly so that we can develop some other options."

UNDERSTANDING FINANCIAL ANALYSIS

There are many different types of financial analysis; each is designed to answer a different set of questions. One type of analysis attempts to determine the profitability of a business and its attractiveness as a potential investment. This is the type of analysis studied here.

The Income Statement

We begin our analysis with an income statement. In its simplest form, an income statement computes the profit of a business for the time period in question—usually one year. Let's take the example of an individual—Bob Jones—who purchases baseball caps for $1 each and sells them for $2. If he buys and sells a thousand hats in 1980, Bob's income statement looks like this:

Bob's Hat Co. 1980

Sales	$2,000	($2 × 1,000)
−Cost of Goods Sold	1,000	($1 × 1,000)
Profit before Tax	$1,000	

Let's suppose Bob is pleased with his profit and hires two people to work for him in 1981. If he hires two employees at $100 each, and they also sell 1,000 hats each (at $2 per hat) his income statement looks like this:

Bob's Hat Co. 1981

Sales	$6,000	(3 × 1,000 × $2)
−Cost of Goods Sold	3,000	($1 × 3,000)
−Salaries	200	(2 × $100)
Profit before Tax	$2,800	

Let's assume that the next year Bob hires three more employees at $100 each, rents an office for $200, spends another $100 on phone calls and typing, and sells 5,000 hats at $2 each. (Now, Bob is just managing the business, not selling any hats himself.) His income statement looks like this:

Bob's Hat Co. 1982

Sales	$10,000	(5 × 1,000 × $2)
−Cost of Goods Sold	5,000	(5 × 1,000 × $1)
−Salaries	500	(5 × $100)
−General and Administrative Expense	100	
Profit Before Tax	$ 4,400	

Note that items like phone calls are termed *General and Administrative Expense*; this will be abbreviated G&A. Also, from now on, Profit Before Tax will be abbreviated PBT and Cost of Goods Sold, COGS.

By this point, we can see how the income statement will look over time. As the business grows, we could keep adding both sales and expenses, and it is hoped, the profit would continue to grow.

Depreciation

There is one item, however, that would make income more difficult to calculate. Suppose Bob bought a $5,000 machine that could make 5,000 hats per year, and the machine was expected to last for five years.

If we followed the process we've been using, we would add an item to the income statement called *machinery expense* and add $5,000 in expenses to this item.

But this would be misleading. We would be charging the business's profits for the whole machine in one year, even though we are using it up over a five-year period. In subsequent years, profits would be overstated because we would be charging the business *nothing* for the machine, even though we were getting the benefit of its hat-producing abilities.

The solution to this problem is to use something called *depreciation*. We only charge the income statement for one-fifth of the machine each year, or $1,000. This one-fifth figure comes from the fact that the machine has a useful life of five years. Thus, at the end of that time we will have charged the business fully for the machine. This $1,000 figure is called depreciation—the machine is getting less valuable each year since we are "using" part of it up (it is the opposite of appreciation). The portion that we use up is called depreciation.

The approach we used above is called *straight-line depreciation*. We simply take the value of the equipment, divide it by the number of years of useful life, and then deduct this much each year from the income statement as depreciation. It is called straight-line depreciation because the value of the equipment decreases by the same amount each year in a straight line. Other forms of depreciation, called *accelerated* methods, deduct proportionally more of the equipment in the earlier years and less later on. For our purposes, we will consider only straight-line depreciation.

If we assume that Bob bought the machine described above, hired five people to run it at $100 per year per person, and the materials for the hat cost 10 cents each, (and that he still had five salespeople working for him at $100 each) then Bob's income statement would look like this:

Bob's Hat Co. 1983

Sales	$10,000	($2 × 5,000)
−COGS	500	($0.10 × 5,000)
−Salaries	1,000	(10 × $100)
−G&A	100	
−Depreciation	1,000	($5,000/5)
PBT	$ 7,400	

Taxes

Up until now, we have been ignoring taxes. Unfortunately, we can't do this in real life. Companies' tax rates, like individuals', vary considerably. For the purposes of this exercise, we will assume that the company pays 40 percent of its income in taxes. In practice, this is a little high for a small company. But it is close enough for our work.

The Uses—and Problems—of an Income Statement

An income statement provides a useful perspective on a business. It allows us to look at how a company's performance changes over time, and how one business compares to another. We can also learn a great deal about the operations of a particular business in a particular year: its sales, expenses, taxes, and profit. The income statement is an important tool that managers often use to run the business. It gives them a great deal of information about the profitability of an operation—where profit is coming from, what the most significant expenses are, and what the most important changes are from one period to the next.

　　The income statement, however, is not a good tool for evaluating whether a business is worth entering in the first place. An income statement does not give us a clear picture of how much cash a business may be throwing off—or using up—in a given year. To do this, we need a cash flow statement. The reasons why are explained below.

Cash Flow

The cash flow of a business is a measure of how much more cash it has at the end of the year t̊ an it did at the beginning. If all of the business's profits went into the bank, the cash flow would be the change in the company's bank balance. But all of the profits from the income statement don't go to the bank. We saw above that we could buy a machine for $5,000 and only charge the business $1,000 on the income statement. The remaining $4,000 still comes out of our cash at the bank, but it does not show up on the income statement. Conversely, in the years after we buy the machine, we will be charging the income statement $1,000 but we will not have paid this in cash—it is just a charge for the portion of the machine that we "used up".

　　We can see how depreciation changes the relationship between the business's income statement and its real cash flow. Until we added depreciation, the income statement was also a cash flow statement; whatever the profit after tax was, this amount was also the cash profit the business had made. Now, when we add depreciation, we see this relationship has changed.

In the first year of the machine's use, cash flow is less than profit because we have a cash outflow of $5,000 to buy the machine, but this appears nowhere on the income statement. The only figure we see is a $1,000 charge for depreciation. In future years, cash flow will be more than profit, because we will be charging the income statement $1,000 in depreciation, but there is no real cash outflow for this.

Thus, we can see there are two components to the differences we are talking about. One is the depreciation figure, and we've seen where that comes from. The other figure is called *investment*—it represents the money spent to purchase equipment. Note that if the company buys something that will be used for more than one year, this is an *investment* and it is depreciated. If the company buys something that it will use up within the year, then this is called an *expense*, and the total amount appears on the income statement. Salaries, G&A, and COGS are expenses. The general formula that converts an income statement to a cash flow statement is:

$$
\begin{array}{l}
 \text{Profit After Tax} \\
+ \text{ Depreciation} \\
- \text{ Investments} \\
\hline
= \text{ Cash Flow}
\end{array}
$$

We can convert Bob's income statements for the first and second years of the machine's life to cash flow statements:

Year	1983	1984
Sales	$10,000	$10,000
COGS	500	500
Salaries	1,000	1,000
G&A	100	100
Depreciation	1,000	1,000
PBT	7,400	7,400
Taxes	3,000	3,000
Profit after Tax	$ 4,400	$ 4,400
+Depreciation	1,000	1,000
−Investment	5,000	—0—
=Cash Flow	$ 400	$ 5,400

This example shows why both the income and cash flow statements provide valuable pieces of information about a business. The income statement indicates the business was just as profitable in 1984 as it was in 1983. From a cash flow perspective, however, the two years are vastly different. There is a severe cash drain on the business in 1983 due to the investment in equipment. In 1984, the business is getting the benefit of that piece of equipment, but does not have to lay out any cash to do so. Depreciation—what the business charged itself to use the equipment—is added back to income and cash flow is higher than profit.

Evaluating Financial Attractiveness

Now that we understand cash flow, we can examine how to analyze financial attractiveness. Let's suppose we were offered the opportunity to buy Bob's business, with the above income statement (for 1984), for $45,000; should we buy it?

There are two questions we would need to consider to make an intelligent decision about the business:

- What is the business's true financial return?
- What return is required to make the investment attractive?

Figuring Financial Return: If we were thinking about buying a business—or even just investing some money in one—the relevant criteria is *return on investment* (ROI). That is, we need to figure out how much money we are putting in, and what we are going to *get out*. In the case of buying Bob's business for $45,000, it's easy to see that $45,000 represents investment, or cash in. Our return on that investment is *not the profit*, but the *cash flow*—this is how much money we would really make if we bought the business. Thus, the ROI on the purchase of Bob's Hat Co. would be 12 percent—or $5,400 divided by $45,000—in 1984.

Another way to look at financial return is "payback." Payback is the number of years it takes to earn all of the original investment back. Thus, if we invested $100,000 in a business, and it had a cash flow of $20,000 per year, it would have a payback of five years.

Note that a higher ROI will always correspond to a shorter payback. These are just two ways of thinking about the same issue.

What Is the Required Return: There are two factors that influence the ROI that we need on an investment in order for it to be considered attractive:

- How risky it is
- What our alternatives are

Risk: It is pretty easy to see why risk is a factor. Think of risk as the probability that we will lose our money. It is easy to see that the higher the risk, the higher the return on our investment must be in order to compensate for taking that risk. If we had a choice between putting our money in a savings bank and earning 12 percent or investing it in Bob's Hat Co., we would probably pick the bank—it is a lot less risky. There is virtually no chance that we would lose our money or that the return would vary.

Alternatives: Similarly, if we had the opportunity to invest in another business of similar risk but that offered a 14 percent return, we would probably invest in that—it is a higher return with no more risk.

Obviously, it is tough to make decisions about investments that offer more risk but also more return. How much more return is sufficient to compensate for the additional risk is a difficult question to answer. Individuals have different risk profiles. People with significant wealth are typically willing to take bigger gambles than those with less financial resources. This makes sense because wealthier people can afford to lose more. Even among individuals with equal wealth, risk profiles vary. Some people are just more willing gamblers than others.

Starting a Business

As we've seen, cash flow equals:

$$
\begin{array}{l}
\text{Income after Tax} \\
+ \text{ Depreciation} \\
\underline{- \text{ Investment}} \\
\\
= \text{Cash Flow}
\end{array}
$$

When beginning a business, we obviously need to determine how much money we will require. There are two components to this need:

- Capital plant and equipment
- Working capital

Plant and Equipment: Money for capital equipment is the most obvious requirement. If we're starting a business, we need to buy the building and machinery with which to manufacture the product. Plant and equipment includes all of these "hard" assets.

Working Capital: Working capital is a less obvious requirement. Working capital refers to the money we will have invested in items like inventory or in cash itself. Working capital is the money we need in order to make money. If we were opening a retail store, for instance, working capital would include the product we had in the store to sell, as well as the cash we would need to run the business—make change for customers, pay employees, buy new inventory, and so on. Obviously, we would hope that the cash coming in from sales would cover the payment of employee salaries. And, on average, it probably would. But we would still want to have a buffer of cash in case we didn't have sufficient sales one week.

Another common instance of working capital is credit. Suppose we bought a truckload of appliances for $100,000 and had to pay for them right away. Now, suppose we sold the appliances for $200,000 the same day, but we sold them on credit. The people who bought them would pay us over the next several months. In this case we would need $100,000 in working capital. It would be the money we needed to run the business. If we could get the person we bought the appliances from to take his money on credit, then we wouldn't need any working capital for this.

Conclusions

The main point of this reading has been to explain *cash flow as the critical piece of data in evaluating the potential attractiveness of a business investment.* An income statement is obviously important, both because it is required to build a cash flow projection and because it presents valuable information. Specifically, we learned:

- How to calculate how much money will be required to start a business—the cash for plant and equipment and working capital
- How to develop projections—from the income statement—that will tell us how much cash flow the business will generate
- How to judge the attractiveness of that cash flow, by comparing to the original investment required, via the measures of ROI or payback

GELATERIA ITALIA (B)

Paula, Mark, and Eric met Saturday morning and pulled together the financial analysis shown in Exhibit 4.1. The students discussed their feelings about what this initial analysis indicated.

Eric: *The projections look good; this is a great business for some-one to invest money in. We shouldn't have any problem raising the capital we need.*

Mark: *That's right, Eric; the projections are attractive. But we still have a lot of issues to resolve regarding how to finance the business. I called the banker yesterday to tell him we were making progress and to suggest that we might come in to talk to him about investing in our business. He explained that banks don't invest money, they loan it. If we need money, we have a choice between selling equity in the business—a piece of ownership of the company—or borrowing the money—taking on debt. Debt is more attractive because it lets us hold on to more of the ownership of the business, but it is riskier because it obligates us to pay interest every month.*

Paula: *That's right. I talked to my father last night, and he said*

Exhibit 4.1   Income and Cash Flow Statements

Income

Revenues	$369,000
COGS	162,000
Wages & Salaries	132,600
Rent	18,720
Advertising & Promotion	5,200
General & Administrative	13,000
Interest	0
Depreciation	19,000
Profit before tax	18,480
Taxes	7,392
Profit after tax	$ 11,088

Cash Flow

Profit after tax	$11,088
+depreciation	19,000
−investments	0
=cash flow	$30,088

These statements were developed based upon the data in the Gelateria Italia (A) case. For instance,

Revenues = ice cream customers × average check = 350 × $1.50 = $525 food customers × food check = 100 × $5.00 = $500 = $1,025 total sales per day × 360 days per year = $369,000 revenues per year *we should try to finance the business with as much debt as possible so that we can maintain most of the equity for ourselves.*

Mark: *That debt could be pretty risky. Don't forget a lot of these numbers are really just assumptions. We really don't have a good idea of what sales are going to be. We will have plenty of fixed expenses in the form of rent and salaries. We don't need to add to our fixed costs with high interest payments.*

Paula: *Well, no matter what we do, we are going to need to pull together a plan to refine our assumptions and present our financing proposal to investors or bankers.*

In the meeting that followed, the three discussed the projections they had developed in the preceding days (see Exhibit 4.1). While they agreed that the projections looked attractive, Paula, Mark, and Eric realized they needed to do a more thorough analysis.

Sources of Financing

Paula, Mark, and Eric had discussed financing, and they each believed they could borrow $5,000 from their parents to contribute as either equity or debt. To raise the remaining funds, they could go to friends and relatives, wealthy individuals, or a bank. Paula came from a fairly wealthy family and said her father had offered to invest up to $25,000 in the business; she indicated he would expect to own a fair amount of the equity in the business for this sizable investment.

Mark had looked into bank financing. The banker had indicated he could not guarantee the company could receive financing. But if they were successful in obtaining bank financing, the most favorable terms they would receive would be:

- A loan in an amount up to 60 percent of the value of the equipment and leasehold improvements
- A 10 percent interest rate

Debt versus Equity

Eric believed they should try to raise the $100,000 in the form of bank debt. This way they could keep 100 percent of the equity for themselves.

Mark was uncomfortable with all bank debt. He said the bankers he had talked to would require them to sign personal guarantees on the debt—that is, if the corporation failed, the banks could come after their personal assets. On the other hand, Mark said he was uncomfortable asking his friends and relatives for money. He said:

Suppose we fail. These people are my friends—they will be important to me the rest of my life. I don't want to jeopardize these relationships over money.

Eric was unhappy with Mark's position:

First you're afraid to borrow money from a bank, and now you don't want to raise money from friends or relatives. We aren't going to make any progress if you keep dragging your feet. There is no way to start a business without taking some risks.

Paula was upset by Mark's reluctance to ask his friends and relatives for money:

I was willing to ask my father for money because I thought that this was important to us. I know it's a risk, Mark, but we should take it—think of the fun we'll have running the business. You seem to have less confidence in us than we have in you.

Mark didn't press his points, and they agreed they would meet the following morning and try to pull the financing plan together.

Paula closed by saying:

We really need to decide how to finance the business—whether the money we raise should be debt or equity. We seem to have different risk profiles, and that is obviously going to influence our point of view. But we should be able to back up our arguments with the numbers. If we run projections of income and cash flow for the different proposals, we can see the effect of different financing decisions.

The students decided they would meet the following morning to finalize their plans.

Mark had a sleepless night, wondering about the future of the business and their relationship:

I started getting a funny feeling in the pit of my stomach. It seemed to me that we had gotten all caught up in the enthusiasm of the project and having our own business. We hadn't been as hard-nosed about the business decisions as we should have been. Our projections are based on Eric standing around an ice cream store. We should do some sort of a market study and go look at some other gelati stores.

I am also concerned about raising $25,000 from Paula's father; that will give her a lot more power than Eric or me. And I already feel like the two of them are ganging up on me. They seem much less risk-averse than I am.

I am also worried about my relationship with Paula and Eric. We are good friends, but that doesn't necessarily make us good partners. Will it really take three of us to run an ice cream store?

Mark's alarm went off. It was time to meet with Eric and Paula.

HOW TO FINANCE A BUSINESS

"Understanding Financial Analysis" described how to use income and cash flow statements to determine the amount of money required to start a business. Once we've determined this, we need to decide where to get it. Possible sources include savings, money obtained from friends or relatives, or money we can borrow from a bank.

In essence, there are only two types of financing: debt and equity. Debt is money we borrow and have to pay back; equity is money that is invested in the company—these investors then own part of the firm. These two types of financing differ in such important respects as:

- The degree of risk each represents to the provider of funds. When we borrow money, we have to agree to pay back both the amount borrowed—the principal—plus interest on that principal, according to a set schedule. If someone provides equity funds, we are not legally obligated to pay them anything. The benefit these equity holders receive is ownership in the firm.

- The degree of risk each represents to the company. Debt is obviously riskier to the company. If we borrow money and don't pay it back, the person (or bank) that lent us the funds can take action. An equity investor has no legal right to payment, so there is little they can do.

- The potential return each offers to the investor. If someone lends our company money, he knows exactly how much he is going to get back and when. The risk is low, but so is the potential return—it is simply the interest on the money. On the other hand, if investors own equity in the company, they have the potential of a very high return—or no return at all. It is this possibility of a high return that gives investors the incentive to bear the risk of an equity investment.

- The cost of each to the company. Debt has a fixed cost—the interest rate we pay to borrow the money is the cost of those funds. Equity, on the other hand, has a variable cost. If we own the company, and if we sell equity to investors, then those investors share in the success of the company. If the company does extremely well and the equity becomes worth a great deal of money, then the investors get some of that money, instead of us getting all of it. Another cost of equity is the control we give up. If investors own equity, they have a right to have a voice in how we run the company.

The following sections will explain each of these points in more detail.

The Firm As Cash Flow

Forget about debt and equity for a minute, and just think about a company. In a financial sense, the company is just a series of cash flows—it is hoped, positive cash flows. In good years, the company

Exhibit 4.2   The Firm's Cash Flow

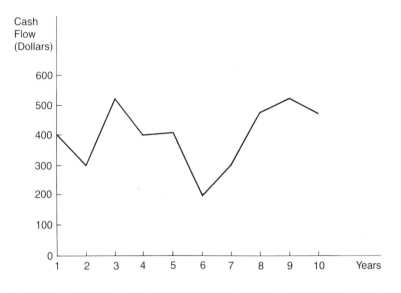

has a high cash flow; it makes a lot of money. In not-so-good years, the company has low cash flow. The company may even have a negative cash flow in a really bad year, but then it can take money out of the bank to make up the difference. The graph in Exhibit 4.2 shows one possible cash flow scenario—a projection—for a company over ten years.

The owners of the company own that cash flow. If we own 100 percent of the company, we have a right to 100 percent of the cash flow. The technical term for ownership of a company is *equity*. Thus, when we buy a share of equity, we buy a share of ownership in the company and a right to that same share of the cash flow. Other terms for owner are *equity holder* or *equity investor*.

Return to the graph above. Suppose the company needed a lot of money to build a new factory—more than it had in the bank. It could *sell a portion of the future cash flow*. This is what a *loan*, or *debt*, is. The company receives, say, $1,000 now, and, in return, has to pay 10 percent interest (after taxes), or $100 per year to the bank (or whoever lent the money). In essence, this cuts off the top piece of the graph. As equity holders, we no longer have a claim on that portion of the cash flow (see Exhibit 4.3).

Conceptually, we could keep selling more and more of this cash flow. But it would keep getting riskier, because every time we borrowed another $1,000, that line on the bottom of the graph would move down $100—magnifying the dip in year six. Remember, this

Exhibit 4.3   The Effect of Debt Financing on Cash Flow

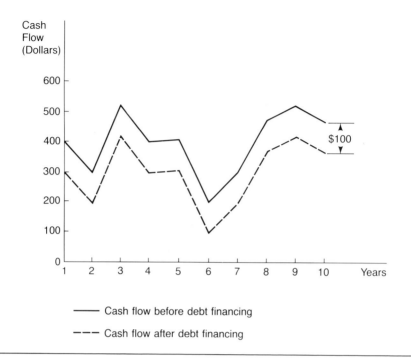

—— Cash flow before debt financing

--- Cash flow after debt financing

graph is a projection. If we miscalculated, and the dip in year six was larger than projected, this would be a year in which we would have a hard time paying our bank loans.

Note that debt is a *fixed* claim on the cash flow—the money we have to pay each year in interest. Equity holders have a claim on the residual cash flow—what's left. In year six above, for instance, the equity holders would get zero.

The equity holders can decide what should happen to this cash flow, whether it should be reinvested in the business or distributed to the equity holders (see more on this topic below).

The following sections give more detail on equity and debt.

Equity

Let's assume we've decided to start a company, and we've determined that $1,000 will be required. If we had $1,000 in the bank (or under a mattress) we could get that money and start a business. That investment of $1,000 would be called *equity capital* for a particular reason:

Technically, equity refers to the ownership of a company. If we

Exhibit 4.4 The Effects of Different Levels of Debt Financing on Cash Flow

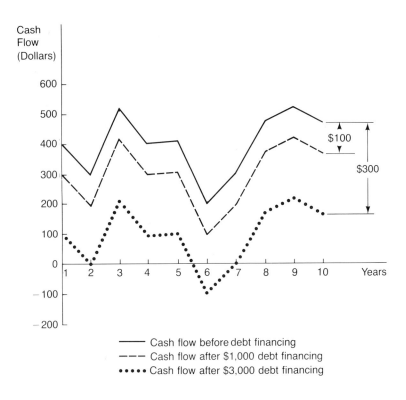

—— Cash flow before debt financing
--- Cash flow after $1,000 debt financing
•••• Cash flow after $3,000 debt financing

buy a share of stock—say in IBM—we are buying a portion of the company's equity. If IBM had 100 shares outstanding and we bought one share, we would one 1 percent. Thus, equity capital brings ownership of the business with it. The control that comes with ownership is exercised by the board of directors, a body of individuals who are elected to represent the shareholders' interests. They are elected by vote of the shareholders. Thus, as an equity owner, you do not necessarily participate in the decision making of the company. Unless you have a seat on the board, you will have a difficult time having a say in the company's affairs.

In this example, if we invested the entire $1,000 the business required, we would own 100 percent of the equity—the entire company. We could decide how many shares we wanted the company to have—10, 100, or 1,000. Whatever number of shares we decided upon, that number would equal 100 percent of the company.

Alternatively, we could sell equity in the business; as discussed

Exhibit 4.5   Debt and Equity Claims on Cash Flow

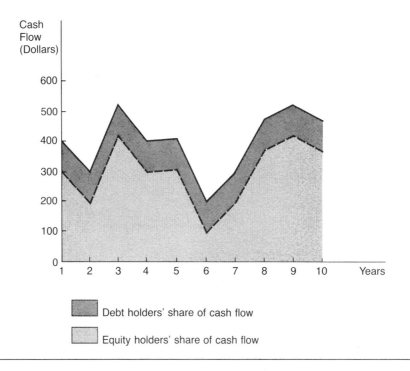

above, this is the equivalent of selling a claim on a portion of the company's cash flow. Suppose we had $100 in the bank; we could go to nine friends and ask them to invest $100 each. In return, they would own some portion of the company's equity—a piece of the company. It is not necessary that they each get the same 10 percent of the company as we did. As the founders, we could argue that we will be doing all the work, as well as contributing some money. Therefore, we would be entitled to a higher percentage, say 20 percent or 30 percent or even 50 percent for our $100. Our friends might argue, and we would have to agree on a fair price for the shares of the company. (Arguing about what percentage of the company a person can buy for $100 is the same thing as arguing about the price of a share of stock. If there are 100 shares, and we argue that $100 buys 10 percent of the company, then we are saying that the price of a share is $10.)

Our friends could pay a higher price for each of their shares than we did, but they would each have to pay the same price as each other. It would be illegal to give some friends a better deal than others.

Obviously, if someone invested money in the company, it would be with the intention of making a profit. Thus, our friends might ask: "If I'm investing $100 for 5 percent of a company, what am I getting in return? How will I ever get my original money, plus a profit back?"

In essence, there are two ways to earn a return on that equity investment:

- Dividends. Dividends are a portion of the cash flow of the company. If the company decided to pay out 100 percent of its cash flow as dividends, then if you owned 5 percent of the company, you would receive 5 percent of its total cash flow as dividends. Most companies don't pay out all of their cash flow in dividends. Just as we don't like to spend absolutely every penny we make in a week, a company likes to save some money for future projects or for a bad year in which it loses money. For example, a company might decide to pay out 50 percent of its cash flow in dividends. If it had a cash flow of $1,000 in one year, and we owned 5 percent, we would get $25. ($1,000 cash flow $\times$ 50 percent pay out $\times$ 5 percent ownership.)
- Sale of stock. The investor could also sell his shares. Of course, it is not clear how much he could sell them for. If the company did well and made a lot of money, the shares could be worth a tremendous amount; if the company did poorly, or even went bankrupt, the shares could be worthless.

Note that if the company keeps some or all of the cash instead of distributing it as dividends, the equity holders are still better off. If the company has more cash in the bank, or if it invests the money in the business to make more money, then—as owners of the business —we are wealthier because the company is worth more. Presumably, if we sold our stock we could get a higher price for it.

Equity capital is also called *risk capital*, and it is easy to see why. When an investor buys equity, he has no way of knowing how much of a return he is going to make on his investment.

Debt

Debt financing is different from equity in that it does not bring ownership of the company with it. On one hand, this is a tremendous advantage to us as the founders. We could get the $1,000 we need to start the company and still own 100 percent of the stock—the equity.

We do, however, have to pay interest on the money we've borrowed. Not only is this a cost, but *it is riskier*. If we borrow money, we are legally obligated to pay the money back according to a set schedule. Remember the graph shown earlier. Borrowing more and more money keeps pushing that line on the graph closer to zero (or negative) cash flow.

Thinking about Risk and Return

In "Understanding Financial Analysis," we looked at financial return as the rate of return on investment (ROI). Now we have to clarify this. We have seen that there are two types of investment—debt and equity.

ROI refers to the rate of return on debt and equity combined. If we are thinking about investing money in a business, however, we are more interested in the rate of return on our own funds—the return on equity, or ROE. Thus, the ultimate measure of a business's performance from the equity owners' point of view is ROE.

We have been thinking about risk as the chance that the company will be unable to meet its interest costs in a given year. One way to quantify this risk is to think of it as the portion of the company's cash flow that has to go to meet these fixed financial obligations. In the case of a firm that is financed with 100 percent equity, we can see that the fixed costs of financing are $0—the firm is not obligated to pay out any of its cash flow. On the other hand, companies financed with debt will have fixed financing costs.

The ratio that captures the risk of the firm's financial structure is called the *debt to equity ratio*. This ratio is calculated by dividing the amount of debt financing by the amount of equity financing. If a company has equal amounts of debt and equity, the ratio is 1 to 1. Because debt has fixed costs associated with it, the higher the proportion of debt, the higher the portion of the company's cash flow that will be allocated to interest payments and the riskier the company will be—remember those graphs and the dip in year six.

If we quantify risk with the debt/equity ratio, what does it actually mean in terms of what could happen to the business? When we borrow money, the bank will want more than our promise to make the business a success. Usually we will have to pledge assets against the loan as collateral. If the business already owns assets—say a building—then the bank will ask that this building serve as collateral against the loan. If the business does not have any assets that can serve as collateral, then the bank may ask us to pledge personal assets, such as a house or a car. The bank would ask us to sign a personal guarantee, which guarantees the loan with our own personal assets.

If the company is unable to meet its obligations, the bank can take drastic measures. These include seizing assets that have been put up as collateral for the loan, forcing the business into bankruptcy or even taking personal assets if we have signed a personal guarantee. The bank can take these actions, but usually doesn't go so far. It has an interest in keeping the business alive so that the business can pay back the money. But it would be unwise to not at least consider these possible consequences.

An Example

To see the effect this financing decision can have on a business, it's instructive to look at an example. Let's take a business that requires $1,000 to start and has the following projected income statement (if financed completely with equity and without any debt):

Sales	$1,000
COGS	600
Salaries	50
G&A	50
Depreciation	100
Profit before Tax	200
Taxes	80
Profit after Tax	120

If we assume that no investment is required beyond the initial $1,000, the cash flow is then:

Profit after Tax	$120
+ Depreciation	$100
Cash Flow	$220

So, the return on investment is 22 percent ($220/$1,000).

If we take the same income statement projections for the business, but now assume that we finance the company by borrowing $500 at 10 percent interest and use only $500 of our own equity, the income statement looks like this:

Sales	$1,000
COGS	600
Salaries	50
G&A	50
Depreciation	100
Interest	50
Profit before Tax	150
Taxes	60
Profit after Tax	90

Now the cash flow is:

Profit after Tax	$ 90
+ Depreciation	100
Cash Flow	190

Even though the cash flow is $30 lower, our return on equity is higher—38 percent ($190/$500) compared to 22 percent ($220/$1,000). This is because our equity investment was *much* lower, only $500.

Let's look at the risk of each of these companies. The "all equity company" has no fixed financing costs, no interest payments, because it is all equity financed. The company that is financed 50:50 with debt and equity, however, has fixed financing costs of $50 per year.

If you were an investor and had the choice of buying 10 percent

of either of the companies described above, which would you buy?
If you bought 10 percent of the all equity company, it would cost you
$100. To buy 10 percent of the company that's financed 50:50 with
debt and equity would cost you only $50. On the other hand, the
company financed with debt and equity will have a lot less money
to pay out in dividends because a lot of its cash flow is going to interest
payments (remember those graphs). And this company is riskier; there
is more of a chance this company could have a bad year and be unable
to meet its interest charges and thus be forced into bankruptcy. It is
not surprising that this company shows a higher rate of return on its
equity—it is riskier, and the equity holders need more return on their
investment to compensate for that higher risk.

Summary

This reading explains the differences between debt and equity. In
starting a business, it is crucial to decide how it is to be financed.
Note that a bank is not the only source of debt. The company can
borrow money from private individuals as well, such as friends and
relatives. Most people starting a business try to get as much debt as
they can. They reason—and rightly so—that the more debt they can
get, the less money they will need to raise by selling equity and the
more equity they can keep. This logic is correct as far as it goes, but
many people neglect to correctly assess the risk of debt.

It is a matter of judgment to decide how much debt is appropriate
for a company. One important factor, though, is how risky the basic
business is. Again, remember those graphs from above. If we were
considering a company that did not have any peaks and valleys in its
cash flow projections, we could feel more comfortable about taking
on the risk of interest payments. On the other hand, if the cash flow
projections for the business have large peaks and valleys, then it becomes very risky to have debt. We don't need to have too much before
we are likely to have a problem paying our interest in a particular
year.

Case 5

Showdown at the Pioneer

Developed by Professor Bert Spector, Northeastern University College of Business Administration, in collaboration with Professor David A. Garvin, Harvard University Graduate School of Business Administration.

It was the evening of August 11, 1986, as Jerry Crockett strolled through the tables of the Mount Hood Holiday Inn dining room to join his party. He was greeted by a number of friends and acquaintances. Crockett was something of a local celebrity because of his position as president of the Pioneer Bank and Trust, and he was enjoying these brief, informal exchanges. Then he spotted a group of employees, several of whom he knew by name, sitting together at a table.

He strolled over and warmly greeted the group and was more than a little surprised when one of them introduced Sharon Landesman, who was also sitting at the table. They didn't have to tell Crockett that Landesman was a regional officer for the Office and Professional Employees International Union (OPEIU), which was attempting to unionize the Pioneer's nonsupervisory employees. The woman looked crisply professional, much closer in appearance, Crockett thought, to a fellow banker than to the few officials from the auto and construction workers' unions with whom he had conducted business. She immediately launched into a pleasant but intense discussion of her union's organizing efforts, including her hope that the bank management would do nothing in the four remaining weeks before the vote that might "jeopardize a constructive relationship" between the Pioneer and the OPEIU in the future.

Landesman's apparent confidence took Crockett aback, and he

felt called upon to express his disagreement. "Oh, I think it will be a relatively close election," he retorted, "but I fully expect that the vast majority of our employees believe that they don't need any *outsiders*"—he paused for emphasis—"to represent them. We're like a family at the Pioneer. And while I'm sure we have problems like any family, most of us feel pretty confident that we can handle those problems ourselves."

"Maybe so," Landesman responded. "But then why do you think it was that nearly three-fourths of your employees signed cards calling for a union election? Why is it that you're so against your employees having a union? What is it that you think they'll get from a union that you don't want them to have? What is it that you're afraid of, Mr. Crockett?"

The Pioneer

The Pioneer first opened its doors in Mount Hood in 1888. As such, it was the town's oldest bank. For nearly three-quarters of a century, Mount Hood remained a small town, relatively isolated from the large city that lay some 20 miles to the northwest. Town merchants and the bank grew together, with the bank financing many of the local businesses and much of the local real estate.

Working at the Pioneer

Over the years, the Pioneer developed a special relationship with its employees. In the 1940s, the bank started an unofficial but well-recognized policy of employment security. Once an employee at any level of the organization made it past the first three years, he or she was virtually guaranteed a job for life (except in cases of dishonesty or blatantly substandard performance). The Pioneer aggressively recruited graduates of the Mount Hood Community College, often financing further college education. Wages at the Pioneer were low: 5 to 10 percent below the other Mount Hood banks and a full 35 percent below the highest paying bank in the nearby city. But benefits were attractive and the 32-hour workweek was considerably shorter than any competitor's. The Pioneer had never had any problems filling its employment needs.

The bank experienced its greatest growth during the 1970s when it considerably expanded the services offered. By 1980 it had amassed assets of $450 million, nearly twice those of either of its two local competitors. But the growth campaign had an impact on bank employees. Previously, bank employees prided themselves on being "one big happy family." All employees, from the president to the maintenance man, knew each other by their first names. The bank building consisted of one large, open room. The president and loan officers conducted all but the most confidential of their business at their regular desks situated directly in the center of the lobby.

Growth considerably increased the number of employees: expanding from 72 in 1970 to 95 in 1975 to 216 in 1982. A complete renovation of the main office soon followed. The lobby was modernized and made more spacious. The second floor, which had been used for storage for as long as anyone could remember, was converted into plush, private offices for the president and all loan officers. One result of the renovation was the movement of the "back office" operation (where checks received by the bank were sorted into individual accounts) into rented office space two blocks from the bank.

The Changing External Environment

Two factors had an important impact on the operations of the bank in the late 1970s and early 1980s: the introduction of new technology and government deregulation.

The Impact of New Technology.   Computer-aided information technology allowed banks, including the Pioneer, to computerize operations previously done manually. The "back room," for instance, was computerized in 1975. Now instead of handling the paperwork for individual accounts and dealing directly with customers concerning problems with accounts or monthly statements, back-room clerks mainly fed data into a computer, ripped the computer-generated statements off the machines, and stuffed envelopes. Those clerk positions were staffed almost entirely by young men who averaged 18 months at the Pioneer before moving to other jobs.

Another major technological change in the banking industry involved the introduction of automated teller machines (ATMs). Customers could now make deposits, withdrawals, or transfers, check balances, and even make small loans with a computer-coded card and an ATM. The machines had several clear advantages. Customers had access to a wide array of bank services 24 hours a day. And although the initial investment in the machines was quite high, they offered the potential of great savings through the reduction in the number of necessary tellers.

Deregulation.   Probably no change shook the banking industry more than deregulation. In the late 1970s President Jimmy Carter and the U.S. Congress moved to introduce competition into previously highly regulated industries: notably commercial aviation and private banking. Jerry Crockett explained the impact of that legislation this way:

Prior to 1980 when deregulation began to take effect, having a bank was pretty much like getting a license to print money. Maybe that's a slight exaggeration, but not much. We all operated on a 3-6-

3 rule: pay depositors 3 percent interest, lend money at 6 percent, and tee off at the golf course by 3 p.m. By gradually deregulating the banking industry through the early 1980s, Congress changed all that; it created a whole new world of banking. As deregulation took hold, there was more competition both among banks and between banks and new entrants such as Merrill Lynch, American Express, even Sears, which will now take the money that individual customers might otherwise have deposited in a bank and "manage" or invest it in such a way as to yield higher interest than we offer on our traditional passbook savings. So now, all our formerly loyal customers are shopping around. They're willing to drive 20 miles for an extra couple of interest points on their savings on certificates of deposits or money market accounts.

The Impact of Deregulation on Employment.   Crockett emphasized that deregulation would have a direct and significant impact on what was expected from employees at the Pioneer:

*What I tell my people, every one of them, is that they have to become a salesperson. If a customer comes in to open a checking account, we have to **sell** that customer a certificate of deposit. If a customer comes in for a mortgage, we have to **sell** them an auto loan as well. I need aggressive people here. And I've told them over and over, no one can come along for a free ride any more.*

These new expectations would be most directly felt in two areas: pay and employment security. Said Crockett:

No more automatic annual raises. We're going to measure everyone's performance, from the teller to the loan officer to the president. Those who perform well are going to be paid well. Those who don't perform well will feel it in their paychecks. Then they have two choices: they can change or they can move on.

I guess I'm implying that the days of having a job guaranteed for life at the Pioneer are over. I haven't said anything officially about that yet, but I'd bet most of my people know it's coming. Our profits are being squeezed, so we have to get our costs down. We just can't afford fat any longer, and the new technology is allowing us all sorts of opportunity to trim that fat.

The Arrival of the OPEIU

Cards calling for an election to allow the OPEIU to represent all nonsupervisory personnel at the Pioneer first appeared in March, 1986. When Jerry Crockett first heard about the cards, he called in all bank officers for a staff meeting. They assured him that the "one big family" atmosphere still dominated the bank. While the union might receive some support in the back room, they doubted that more than 10 percent of the tellers would sign cards. "Our people think of unions as cigar-chomping, beer guzzlers with dirt under their fingernails," insisted Alan Lanis, a loan officer. "Plus," said Karen Larson, a supervisor, "a lot of our people, particularly the young men, want to be loan officers and vice-presidents themselves some day. They already think of themselves as 'management,' certainly not as 'laborers.' "

Background on Union Organizing Campaigns

The process of deciding whether to have a union represent employees is known as an organizing campaign. In most cases, that campaign starts only after a union has been invited in by one or more of the company's employees. A professional union organizer, with the help of those employees, then asks other employees to sign a card asking that an election be held in which employees would have the option of voting for that union or for no union. Under federal law the union must secure the signatures of at least 30 percent of the employees. In the election, employees who signed cards are still free to vote either for or against union representation.

If most of the employees vote for no union, the organizing campaign ends. If most of the workers vote yes, the union becomes the authorized bargaining agent for all the eligible workers (not just those who voted yes). At that point, union and management are required to enter negotiations. However, by appealing through the federal court system, management may actually delay entering into negotiations for as long as a year.

Management Responds

Crockett accepted the confident assessment of his staff and took no steps until the afternoon of July 2. Then he received a registered letter from Sharon Landesman, regional director of the OPEIU, informing him that the union had received signed cards from 73 percent of the Pioneer's nonsupervisory personnel. Crockett immediately phoned Jim Halter, a tennis partner and local labor lawyer.

"I have to be honest with you, Jim," Crockett said. "I've never had much experience with unions and I don't know much about them."

"Here's what I'll do," replied Halter. "I'll write you a memo that will be a crash course on what unions are all about (see Exhibit 5.1). What you've got to be careful of, though, is to avoid anything that might be considered an unfair labor practice. If the National Labor Relations Board decides that you've done anything that might interfere with an employee's right to make a free choice, they could just declare the union in without even holding the election. You can't threaten or coerce employees in any way. Don't threaten any reprisals like losing your job or cutting your benefits if you support the union. Likewise, make sure you don't offer them anything extra like more money or benefits if they vote against the union."

"It doesn't sound like there's much I can do," protested Crocket.

Exhibit 5.1   Background on U.S. Trade Unions

TO: Jerry Crockett, President
           Pioneer Bank and Trust
FROM: James Halter, Attorney

What Are Unions?
     Unions are associations of employees that seek to bargain as a
group with employers over conditions of employment. The presence
of unions often results in higher wages as compared with nonunion
operations in the same industry, but also often in lower turnover of
employees and, as a result, higher productivity. Union activities are
regulated and protected by a web of federal laws, most notably the
National Labor Relations Act (1935), which recognized the right of
workers to organize into unions that can bargain over such issues as
wages, hours, and other conditions of employment. It guaranteed employees the right to select any union of their choice. And it made any
attempt by employers to dominate or otherwise interfere with the
formation or administration of any labor organization an unfair labor
practice. Finally, the act created the National Labor Relations Board
(NLRB), a five-member independent federal agency appointed by the
president to oversee proper functioning of the law's provisions and
to issue rulings and directives.

The Content of Collective Bargaining
     Once employees have voted in favor of having a union represent
them, management and the union are required by law to bargain
together. The content of union-management negotiations usually cen-
ters around three considerations:

1. Actual wages of union members.
2. Benefit plans such as vacation and vacation pay, holidays and
   holiday pay, and fringe benefits.
3. Conditions of employment such as how specific jobs will be
   defined (who does what work), discipline and discharge, promotions and demotions, layoffs, seniority rights, job safety, and
   procedures for handling worker-supervisory disputes.

     If negotiations between union and management fail to achieve
a mutually acceptable agreement, the union is free to strike and management is free to replace striking employees. Throughout the 1960s
and 1970s, the percentage of workdays lost to strikes was exceedingly
small—about 0.2 percent—although still quite costly for individual
companies.

Exhibit 5.1 *continued*

Unions and White-Collar Workers

Unions have traditionally been associated with craft and industrial workers. The largest national unions—the Teamsters, the United Auto Workers, and the United Steelworkers—are made up almost exclusively of industrial or blue-collar workers. White-collar workers (office and professional workers) were thought to be resistant to the appeal of unions for several reasons. First, their relatively higher position in the organization was thought to give them more influence than blue-collar workers over their working conditions. Also, they were more likely than blue-collar workers to identify with management and to view unions as "rabble-rousing" organizations beneath their dignity. As a result, unionization among office workers was quite low: only 10 to 11 percent as of 1980.

But important changes in the American economy have led at least some unions to reconsider that traditional reluctance. The decline of American manufacturing in the 1970s reduced manufacturing jobs from 34 percent of the work force in 1950 to 23 percent in 1980. At the same time, white-collar jobs rose dramatically: by 1980 more than half of all employees held office jobs. The percentage of workers belonging to a union dropped along with the decline of manufacturing. Just after World War II 36 percent of the work force belonged to a union. By 1970 that number had dropped to 30 percent and then to just under 20 percent by 1985.

As a result of these trends, a number of union leaders began to realize that future growth depended upon their ability to reach traditionally reluctant white-collar workers. A spokesperson for the Teamsters noted, "The white-collar worker is coming around to realize that while he or she may be enjoying titles and so-called professionalism, the guy in the warehouse is earning more money." And Sharon Landesman of the OPEIU put it bluntly: "The future of the trade union movement is with white-collar workers."

"That's just not so," answered Halter. "You've got every right to oppose that union as vigorously as you can. You can tell your employees why you think they're better off without a union. Warn them that the union will promise them all sorts of things during the campaign—higher wages, job security, anything—but that doesn't mean they'll actually get it. The union still has to negotiate with management. Tell them that if the union takes them out on strike, they'll lose wages they can never make up. And the bank could lose customers that they'll never replace. Tell them they don't need any union grievance procedures to settle disputes; if they ever have any problems with their supervisors or anything else on the job, your door is always open. In other words, they have lots to lose and nothing to gain from joining a union."

"I guess what bothers me the most," said Crockett, "is what if the union *does* win? Won't running a tough, anti-union campaign start off future union-management relations on the wrong foot? We'd already be at each other's throats before we ever sat down at a negotiating table."

"Jerry," Halter answered. "You run a good, tough, legal campaign and you won't have to deal with a union—ever."

Just 48 hours after Crockett received the memo from his lawyer, he sent a letter to every employee at the Pioneer (see Exhibit 5.2). Beyond that, Crockett took no direct steps. Instead, he urged all of his officers, especially those who directly supervised employees who would be voting, to get his message across: it's never been necessary in the past to have a union, and it certainly is not necessary now.

Employee Response to the OPEIU

Four employees of the Pioneer talked in some detail about their feelings on the upcoming vote:

Tom Spiro, Back-Room Clerk.   Spiro, age 21, has been working at the Pioneer for two and a half years:

One morning when I got to my desk, I found this blue card on it. I had no idea what it was all about, but the guy sitting next to me told me it was for a union so we could get paid better. I signed the card and so did everyone in the "sweatshop"—that's what we call our room here.

To be honest, I don't care much about it one way or the other. I'm just killing time here until my cousin can get me on at the GM plant up in Columbia where the pay is really good. I'll join a union there because I have to, but it doesn't matter much to me here.

We all had a good laugh, though, when we got this letter from the bank president. "Dear Friend." That's how it started. Went on to say what a great place the Pioneer is to work for; about how all 216 of us employees are "bankers" working for Mount Hood's best bank. I mean—come on. I'm no banker. I work in a big room over a donut shop with 11 other people. Forget all this prestige stuff. How about some more in our weekly paycheck? Do you have any idea what those guys up at GM make?

Then he goes on to say how we don't need any outsiders from a union telling us how to run our business; that if we have any problems, we should feel free to come in and talk with him personally. His door is always open. Now that's the real laugh. I've been in that bank once; the day I interviewed for my job. I don't even bank here. I bet if I walked into the bank and tried to go upstairs to talk with the president, I'd get thrown right out. Don't you think?

Exhibit 5.2   Letter From Jerry Crockett to Pioneer Employees

Jerry Crockett, President
Pioneer Bank & Trust
July 6, 1986

Dear Friend:

I'd like to take this opportunity to speak directly to each and every one of you. I am aware, as I am sure you all are, of recent efforts to bring a union into our Pioneer Bank family. While I have no intention of trying to tell you how to vote, I wanted there to be no doubt in your mind of how I feel about the bank and its employees.

The Pioneer has long been one of the premier banking establishments not just in Mount Hood but also in the entire state. We have become an important, profitable institution in our community not because of me or any other individual who has occupied my office. It has always been *you*, the members of the Pioneer family, who have made this institution a great one. In turn, the bank has treated all its employees well. Our pay, benefits, and working conditions have always been excellent. (No bank in the state can match our educational benefits or flexible work hours!) I suppose like any family, we have our problems here from time to time. But we sure don't need outsiders telling us how to deal with those problems. My door is always open to each and every one of you. Together, we can work out any problems we might have.

We have not made the Pioneer such a fine place to work by accident. Bank management has made the Pioneer what it is because we *care* about each and every one of you. There is no "us" and "them" at the Pioneer. We're *all* bankers, *all* part of the Pioneer family. It is my sincerest hope, and my pledge to you, that this spirit will stay alive at the Pioneer.

Sincerely,
Jerry Crockett

So I don't really know what I'll do about the election. What I want to do is keep to myself and stay out of trouble. If I'm lucky, I won't even be here by the time the election comes around.

Ricky Mink, Teller.   Mink, 24, started working at the bank five years ago after graduation from Mount Hood Community College. With the Pioneer paying for his education, he completed a B. A. degree and was planning on enrolling in an M. B. A. program at the nearby state university:

I guess I'm one of the few people who didn't sign a union card. I've always thought unions were for auto workers, truck drivers, people like that. Plus, the bank's been good to me. I've been told, informally, that within six months, I'll be doing mortgages, then commercial loans. I'm being groomed. I ran into Jerry Crockett the other day in the little coffee room we have here. Not only did he know my name, but he asked me about school and brought up my transfer to mortgage. That's pretty impressive. Besides, I don't think the bank would be encouraging me to get an M. B. A. unless they thought I was vice-presidential material, do you?

Sandra Smith, Teller.   Smith, 47, came to the Pioneer ten years ago and had been working as a teller ever since:

I guess I have a somewhat different view of things than Ricky. Nobody is grooming me to be vice-president or anything else. But I probably would have been perfectly happy staying a teller here. The pay isn't all that great, but the benefits are good and the hours are terrific. But things are changing. For one thing, there are rumors all over the place that we're going to a 40-hour workweek. One of the women who just got hired said that's what the personnel person told her.

Then, too, our pay system just changed. It used to be if you did your job well and stayed out of trouble, you'd get a regular raise. Now we've gone to what they call merit pay. A lot of us are worried about that. What's going to happen to our raises? With our supervisor rating us, it will probably turn into a popularity contest anyway. If you get along with her, you'll do fine. If not, look out.

But I guess what has us most worried is all these ATMs. We got into that a few years back, but not nearly as much as some of the other banks. But it's coming. And what does that mean for us tellers? There's a rumor that the Pioneer wants to open a branch up the highway with just a few vice-presidents and a bunch of machines. I don't know if that's true or not, but there is one thing I'm sure of: the machines aren't going to replace vice-presidents, they're going to replace us.

Anyway, I signed a union card. But, to tell you the truth, I'm not sure how I'm going to vote. My big question is: what can the union do about any of this? Look at what goes on at that GM plant up in Columbia. They lay off people there every year it seems. The union doesn't do much to help them. And twice that I can remember, the union took them out on strike, once for two months. I guess they ended up with a little bit more money in their paychecks. But I know I couldn't afford to be out of work that long. So I just wonder. Will having a union in the Pioneer make things any better, or just make them worse?

Linda Fried, Bookkeeper, Commercial Loan Department.   Fried, 57, started with the bank the day after graduation from Mount Hood's old two-year college.

I've been at the Pioneer over 35 years and worked in nearly every department there is. I started out as a teller just like everybody else, but pretty soon I was doing loans. In those days, we didn't have one vice-president for mortgages, another one for small business, and so on. There was just one fellow who sort of supervised all the loans, and then the rest of us who did all the work. I sat at a desk right out in the center of the lobby. Any customer who walked through the door could talk to me: a young couple looking for a mortgage, parents who needed money for their kids' schooling, somebody wanting to start a hardware store in Mount Hood. You name it, I did it. I talked with them, and if I thought they could handle the payments, I walked right up to the president's desk—that's when it was just three desks down from my own—and had him sign the note. He didn't spend much time on it. If it was all right with me, it was all right with him, and he'd sign. Then he'd walk over and shake the customers' hands, and that was that.

That's all changed now. First, we have those vice-presidents we had to go through. No more walking into the president's office. Once he moved upstairs, we hardly ever saw him. And then we had to specialize: you either did mortgages or commercial loans, but not both.

*I guess I'd have to admit I was getting bored and a bit frustrated. It just didn't seem like I was very important around here anymore. So when the union cards showed up, I was willing to listen. Maybe **they** could get the men who run this bank to understand that a lot of us feel the same way, feel like things at the bank are kind of passing us over. And I was real excited at first. Particularly when Sharon Landesman showed up. I was expecting—you know—something different. She's a professional woman, just like us. But lately, I've been a bit disappointed. Mostly, Sharon's been talking about getting us more money and making sure those automated teller machines don't take away our jobs. But I'm not unhappy with our pay and I think the bank needs more automation to compete. I'm sure not worried about losing my job. I want to know what the union's going to do about how dull our jobs have become and about how nobody listens to us much any more.*

The Next 30 Days

After his brief run-in with Sharon Landesman at the restaurant, Crockett returned to his office rather than to his home. It was now clear to him that he had underestimated the OPEIU's appeal to his employees. He wondered if he could afford to remain so aloof from the "battle." He took out a sheet of yellow legal paper and wrote the word "Actions" in big black letters at the top. What steps could he take in the remaining month?

Crockett remembered Jim Halter's suggestion that he get tough to make sure that the union did not win. But what did *get tough* mean? Legally, he couldn't threaten anybody or even make any promises about what he would do for employees if they voted down a union. Maybe he could hint that certain benefits might be taken away? How about the 40-hour workweek? That was an idea he had floated long before the OPEIU cards showed up. Just maybe he could get away with that. Maybe it was time for another letter, this time tougher. Maybe he could scare people a little, talk about strikes and how they could lose pay, even their jobs. That certainly wouldn't violate any laws. But was it too late for letters? How about a more positive approach, perhaps meeting directly with employees, either in departments or all together. But what would he say? He better have a good answer when Landesman's question—why are you so afraid of a union—got raised by his employees.

Then Crockett thought of the question he had asked Jim Halter. What if he got tough and the union did win? What then? He could take the election to court and stall them for another year. But eventually he'd have to sit at a table and deal with them. Did he really want the union to be an enemy? Did he really have any choice?

Instead of answers, Crockett kept thinking of new questions. What if he fought the union hard and won? Jim Halter would be happy because we beat them. But what about me and my supervisors? I have to live with these people after the election. How do I make sure my employees don't feel like they've been beaten down by management?

Crockett had no answers yet. Instead, he tore off a second sheet and wrote the word "Consequences" at the top. The only thing he was sure of now was that for every action he decided to take, he would be sure to consider the consequences of that action.

Sharon Landesman returned to her office after dinner as well. She was concerned that the OPEIU was not getting through to many of the employees; she might even be losing some of them. She was confident that the union would receive overwhelming support in the back room. But what about the tellers? What could she say to Ricky Mink, who already thought of himself as management? And what about Sandra Smith? What could the union do about merit pay or the new ATMs? But most disturbing was Linda Fried. Her concerns were less tangible than the others, yet she had asked the toughest question of all: what could the union do for her?

Case 6

The Norton Company: Managing Change and Changing Management

Developed by Dr. Artemis March, associate for case development, Harvard University Graduate School of Business Administration, in collaboration with Professor David A. Garvin, Harvard University Graduate School of Business Administration.

THE NORTON COMPANY: MANAGING CHANGE AND CHANGING MANAGEMENT (A)

Once a year, the Norton Company's Organic Grinding Wheel Division shut down its two Worcester, Massachusetts, plants for the day to recognize the accomplishments of the 175 people involved in its Quality Circle[1] (QC) program and to think about improvements for the coming year. (See Exhibit 6.1 for an organization chart and Exhibit 6.2 for the QC operating policies.) Each circle discussed what it had been doing, and Joe Paterno, vice-president and general manager of the division, reaffirmed his commitment to the program:

*Corporate has been exploring ways to cut costs, so that had led some people to ask, "Can we afford Quality Circles?" I said to them the same thing I said when that question came up during the '82 recession: "Can we afford **not** to have them?" As far as I'm concerned the QC facilitator has the safest job in our division.*

During dinner, several people commented on QC's impact on the division:

Ed Sadowski, general foreman for large wheel finishing:

---

[1] Quality Circles consisted of groups of five to ten people doing similar work who met regularly to identify, analyze, solve, and implement solutions to work-related problems. Each circle had a leader to coordinate its meetings and activities. All the circles in a QC program were coordinated by a single individual, called a *facilitator*, who also trained leaders and acted as a resource and guide on the circles' processes, problems, and activities. Responsibility for the program was lodged in a steering committee, usually composed of 10 to 12 people from different departments and levels in the organization. Exhibit 6.2 elaborates some of these roles, responsibilities, and policies Grinding Wheel used to run its program.

Exhibit 6.1 Organizational Chart (Partial)

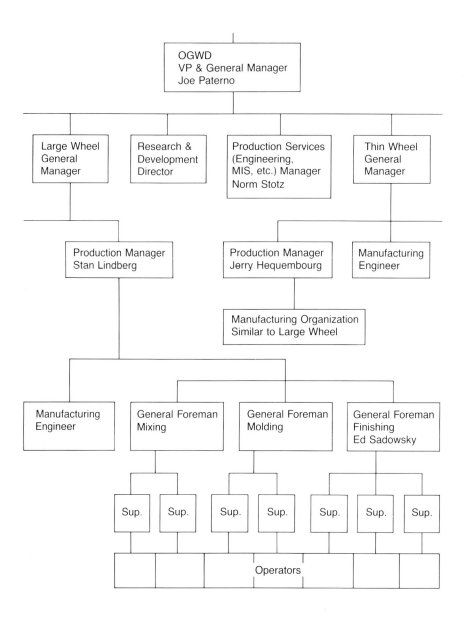

Exhibit 6.2   Quality Circles Operating Policy for Employees of OGWD[a]

1.0   Responsibility

    1.1   Circle Member

        A.   Participation in a Quality Circle is totally voluntary.

        D.   Members are trained to learn problem-solving techniques and apply them to both circle activities and their job.

        E.   Members are expected to be active and support their circle by attending circle meetings, offering ideas, and participating in circle activities.

        F.   Members are expected to present circle recommendations to the appropriate management.

        G.   Members are asked to identify, analyze, and, when possible, implement and monitor solutions to problems in their work area.

    1.2   Circle Leader

        A.   Encourage member participation, open and effective communications, and develop the talent of the circle's members.

        B.   Train members.

        C.   Prepare and conduct circle meetings and coordinate the activities of an individual circle.

        E.   Act as liaison to other departments and support personnel.

        F.   Know how to get things accomplished with the present organization.

        G.   Make judgment as to the appropriate management to present project material to.

    1.3   Facilitator

        A.   Train circle members and assist circle leaders in training members.

        B.   Meet with circle leaders during the training phase before each meeting to discuss the subject and review the lesson plan. After the training phase, the facilitator must ensure that the leaders are always prepared for their meetings.

        C.   Interface between circles, the steering committee, and if required, other individuals and groups within the company.

        D.   Locate specialists who will assist a circle on a particular problem.

        H.   Be available to meet and talk with the circle leader or members outside the confines of the circle meeting.

        J.   Monitor and report circle and member effectiveness.

    1.4   Steering Committee

        A.   Establish and approve the Quality Circle policies, procedures, and objectives.

        B.   Provide guidance and direction to the Quality Circle program.

        C.   Serve as mediator for any problems encountered by the Quality Circle program.

        D.   Show support of Quality Circle and leader by actions.

        F.   Monitor circle effectiveness.

        G.   Responsible to the vice-president and general manager of OGWD and to the general operating policies and philosophies of the corporation.

    1.5   OGWD Management

        A.   Be openly supportive of the circles by actions.

        B.   Provide resources required to conduct effective meetings.

        C.   Allow company time weekly (usually one hour) for circle meetings.

        D.   Select the areas where new circles should be formed, define the bounds of the areas, set the maximum size of the circle, and select the circle leaders.

2.0   Goals

    2.1   To improve communications between all employees at all levels.

    2.2   To develop and use skills of the employees of OGWD.

    2.3   To allow circle members to recommend solutions to problems in their work environment.

    2.4   To promote the feeling of contribution, understanding, and involvement in the business of OGWD.

    2.5   To improve quality, productivity, and working conditions by finding solutions to problems affecting OGWD.

    2.6   To contribute to the long-term financial success of OGWD and its employees.

Figure 6.2 *continued*

3.0   Procedures
    3.6   Selection of Projects
        A circle project may originate from circle members, management, staff personnel, or other circles. By discussion within the circle, the circle selects a project to work on and the leader will advise the facilitator of the choice.
        Circles may not work on projects related to the following:
            a.   Salaries and benefits
            b.   Company policies
            c.   Personalities
    3.7   Member Training
        Training, as provided in Quality Circles, is a continuing experience and involves learning how to apply the techniques used to identify, analyze, and solve work-related problems. Presentation techniques and tools on selling solutions (solution justification) will also be taught when appropriate.
    3.8   Management Presentations
        A.   A circle may make a presentation to management to:
            a.   Show results of completed projects
            b.   Make recommendations and get approval for problem solutions
            c.   Provide status on long-term projects
            d.   Provide status on current circle topics
        B.   If the circle's recommendation for solving a problem requires funding, the presentation is made to that level of management authorized to approve the funds required.
        C.   If a solution requires no funding, if it is a status report, or if it is a report on a completed project, the presentation is made to the superintendent of the affected area for a manufacturing project or to the department manager for a nonmanufacturing project.

ªAbbreviated and reprinted with permission from Norton Company.

When I first came here, if the boss said, "Do this," I did it. If I said, "How come?" the answer was, "Because I told you so." Now, if you ask, "How come?" you get an answer.

Stan Lindberg, production manager for large wheel:

Participative management is not the easiest way to do things, but it is the most effective. It's easier to say, "Do this." But saying, "Here's a problem; what do you think?" will get you further in the long run.

Billy Balunis, quality control inspector, formerly a materials handler:

People have a little more say than in the past, though there's no drastic change. You're more listened to through QCs. You can get things down through a QC; if the idea is sound, management will adopt it.

Don Bianchini, original QC facilitator, now a general foreman:

Improved communications is our number one accomplishment. Employee-management relations were not good before the program, but now people have the satisfaction of feeling listened to and of seeing their ideas implemented. People even come in when they're on vacation or layoff to work on their presentations. It's tremendous to see this kind of attitude change.

Joe Paterno:

The cost savings have been substantial, but if you added those up and compared them with the total hours of lost production and other QC costs, I think it would be a wash. What's really clear is that people feel better about their jobs, and that they're being asked and allowed to contribute.

Norton Company

Products.   During the past century, the Norton Company had developed and manufactured abrasives that could cut, shape, grind, and smooth any material, including steel, glass, ceramics, and plastics. While the company had expanded into other products, abrasives remained its core business. Norton had also developed much of the manufacturing technology for turning its powdered abrasives into grinding wheels, the form in which it sold many of its abrasives.

Competition.   The company had long been a leader in its markets. In the 1980s, however, growth had flattened in some markets, and Norton faced tougher price competition from both domestic and foreign producers. Norton's response was threefold: 1) continue to produce a full line of abrasives, 2) continue to work closely with customers to raise the performance of old products and tailor new ones to their needs, and 3) streamline operations and introduce programs to cut costs.

Organic Grinding Wheel Division

Products and Competition.   Organic Grinding Wheel Division (GW) was one of Norton's abrasives divisions, so named because it used organic binders to hold together the abrasives in its wheels. In the 1980s, both of Grinding Wheel's basic product lines, large wheels and thin wheels, faced greater cost competition. Large wheels, which contained costly materials and engineering time, were sold primarily on the basis of performance, i.e., they did something important and/or unique for the customer's product. Thin wheels, whose major cost component was labor, were much less sensitive to performance requirements and much more sensitive to cost competition.

Work Force and Management Style.   The pre-QC work environment in GW was described by Ed Sadowski, general foreman of thin wheel finishing: "A lot of us were 'Theory X' managers, not just in Grinding Wheel, but in all of Norton. I worked for Theory X people, and invariably it rubs off." (See Exhibit 6.3 for an explanation of Theory X and Theory Y approaches to management.) Though not unionized, jobs were spelled out in detail, giving each worker limited scope of activity. Jerry Hequembourg, production manager of thin wheel, acknowledged the consequences: "People were bored with their repetitious jobs. We had a lot of people on our shop floor with bachelor's and associate's degrees, but they were not being asked to think and

---

Exhibit 6.3   Theory X and Theory Y Management

Theory X and Theory Y were terms coined in the 1950s by Douglas McGregor to describe two styles of management.[a] Each style made different assumptions about employees and about the kind of management required to motivate them to work. Today these terms have become so common that they are routinely used by managers, supervisors, and workers at GW to discuss work environments.

Theory X: This traditional style of management assumed employees were inherently lazy, unwilling to work and to accept responsibility. Therefore, to get work out of them, close supervision and tight control were needed. Since workers were passive, management had to actively direct, reward, and punish their activities. Theory X management assumed that money was the major way to motivate performance.

Theory Y: This style of management explained uncooperative, minimal performance not as part of human nature but rather as the predictable response of employees to being managed in ways that ignored important needs. Theory Y drew on work in psychology that argued people have different levels of needs, and when the lower levels were satisfied, they no longer acted as motivators. Higher level needs then emerged and became active as motivators. When applied to the work environment, this theory suggested that as financial needs were met, more money was not an adequate motivator for high performance. Instead, social needs for belonging and acceptance, and ego needs for competence, achievement, and recognition became more significant as motivators. Yet most organizations offered few such opportunities to people in the lower levels of the organization.

Theory Y assumed that people wanted to do good work and were usually blocked from doing their best by organizational and management practices. Rather than directing and controlling, management's job was removing obstacles, creating opportunities, and providing guidance. In this way, it could harness the higher level needs of its people to achieving organizational objectives.

---

[a]Douglas McGregor, "The Human Side of Enterprise," *Sloan Management Review* 46 (1957).

---

had little opportunity to make a difference." Workers typically felt, "I'm here to do a job; I just do what I'm told." When a piece of equipment broke or an order was lost, the prevailing attitude was, "That's not my job." Workers waited for plant engineers to fix equipment and left it to others to track lost parts or push late orders through.

About the only way workers' ideas were tapped was a company-wide suggestion system. After filling out a form detailing the problem and suggestion, the worker waited weeks or months to hear from the group that evaluated suggestions. Hequembourg described the shortcomings of this system:

If they hit the bull's-eye with their suggestions, they might get a reward up to $5,000. But if the answer was no, they didn't understand why because they hadn't seen it tried. The system was too rigid and it discouraged some people, who then gave up trying.

Beginnings of Change.   During the 1970s, GW took a few small steps to open communication between management and hourly employees. Then at the end of 1980, Joe Paterno was named head of the division. He focused on developing higher value, differentiated products and on cutting costs. He was also a believer in participative, or Theory Y, management (see Exhibit 6.3) and wanted to start a Quality Circle program to move GW in that direction. He recalled:

I saw QCs as a way to get our blue-collar people more involved in the business. I was also very motivated by the cost-savings potential. Some people wanted to push one purpose or the other, but I wanted both. Our work force would not have allowed us to paint too altruistic a picture anyway—they are too sharp.

Quality Circles

In Japan, where QCs had originated, they were used to complete rather than begin a process of quality improvement. This was based on the view that most quality problems were embedded in the business systems—the practices and procedures through which the company or division operated. These included its choice of manufacturing technology, work force policies, the quality of raw materials or components purchased, and so on. The Japanese believed that management, not individual workers, had responsibility for changing these systems. In this view, QCs should emerge only after management had taken care of systemic problems. In the United States, by contrast, QC programs were more likely to be used by themselves, in place of a statistically based quality program, or as the first step in such a program. They were also less likely to be confined to quality issues, and had been used as mechanisms for introducing or increasing participative management, for enhancing the quality of work life, for improving communication, for raising employee morale and commitment, and for achieving cost savings as well as for improving quality.

Steps in Launching a QC Program in GW

Paterno wanted to make sure GW got its program off to a good start. "After all," he commented, "you can only raise the soufflé once." He decided to use outside consultants who had expertise in QCs to provide a framework for launching the program and to work closely with GW to get it started.[2] He chose the Center for Manufacturing Productivity, a group at Rensselaer Polytechnic Institute (RPI).

Steering Committee and Facilitator.   First, a steering committee was formed to define QC objectives and manage the overall effort. (See Exhibit 6.2.) Members included both production managers, the heads of production and of research and development, a supervisor, two hourly employees, two human resources people from corporate, and, as soon as he was chosen, the facilitator. Paterno insisted the facilitator be a full-time position. When it was posted, 38 people applied. The steering committee looked for someone with strong people skills, shop floor credibility, and experience leading groups. After extensive interviewing, Don Bianchini was selected. Bianchini, who had spent several years on the shop floor before becoming a substitute super-

---

[2]Consultants provide services and expertise to companies during a limited time period for an agreed-upon fee. The contract specifies the range of activities to be performed by the consultant.

visor, was very enthused about the program and viewed it as an opportunity to "open more doors" if he succeeded in this new role.

Selling the Program.   Bianchini, the RPI consultants, and the steering committee members met with supervisors to describe the program and its benefits and to deal with their objections and concerns. They looked for supervisors who already leaned toward a participative style, and who embraced the program. Bianchini was candid about the choice of QC leaders: "We wanted to stack the deck for success, so we hand-picked people who had already demonstrated they could work on a team." They also brought employees together in the cafeteria, and met in small groups as well, to discuss quality circles. The division newsletter carried items about the new program, and all employees received a letter sent to their homes from the then-plant manager describing the program and its purposes. (Exhibit 6.4 is a copy of the letter.) Following a publicity campaign, sign-up lists were posted on the bulletin boards. Enough interest was generated in the voluntary program to start five circles by November 1981.

Training.   Bianchini devoted much of his time to training. After being trained himself as RPI, he and the consultants trained the QC leaders and then worked with the leaders to train their members. As the program took hold, he continued to coach leaders on running effective meetings in a participatory manner. He sat down with them before weekly meetings to critique the prior meeting and discuss the structure and agenda of the upcoming meeting. He also attended most circle meetings and coached members on presentation skills.

Early Reactions

Paterno had quickly gained the support of his top managers for the program. General foremen were less enthused, and at least one, Sadowski, thought "it was one of those 'motherhood phrases' that would never fly." He continued:

*But since it was presented to us as something we **are** going to do, we didn't have a lot of choice. I thought, "Well, we'll try it." I told my people, "This is your chance to put up or shut up. This could improve your work life and help our department."*

Sadowski was concerned that supervisory presence might intimidate other circle members, and he preferred his supervisors not be involved in the program for this reason. But Bianchini and the steering committee recognized that for the program to be successful, it was critical that first-line supervisors be brought on board.

Selling to Supervisors.   Bianchini found his biggest selling point with supervisors was that QCs would make their jobs easier because "12 people won't be bugging you all day." Employees would solve more

Exhibit 6.4   Letter to OGWD Employees

NORTON COMPANY WORCESTER, MASSACHUSETTS 01606 · AREA CODE 617 853-1000

To: All Employees of OGWD   October 1, 1981

As many of you have already heard, Quality Circles are to
be introduced into OGWD in the very near future. Don
Bianchini was recently selected as Quality Circle Facilitator
from a group of applicants from within Norton and he will
be working in the coming months to prepare OGWD for the
introduction of the circles. A steering committee composed
of Norton personnel and supported by staff from RPI will
assist Don in the implementation.

What Is A Quality Circle?

Basically, a Quality Circle is a method for improving
communication between people at all levels of OGWD. Circles
give employees an opportunity to contribute their knowledge
to the identification and solving of problems which they
feel are interfering with their own effectiveness on the job.
Members have the chance to not only improve their work place,
but also to work as a team to better their own skills in
communication, data analysis, and problem solving. Within
the last ten years, Quality Circles have been introduced
and proven very successful in corporations such as Boeing,
Honeywell, GM, and GE. I'm confident that they will be
just as successful in Norton.

How Do Quality Circles Work?

A Quality Circle consists of 5 to 15 employees who are located
in the same general area and do similar work. Membership is
on a strictly voluntary basis and participants who choose
to leave the group may do so at any time. One member of the
group, typically the foreman, serves as leader of the group,
training members in problem-solving techniques as the need
arises. Circle members meet for approximately one hour per
week, normally during regular working hours, to discuss
problems they have come across in their own working areas.
However, the activity of the circle is not limited to problem
identification. Circle members also work as a group to
improve the work environment by determining solutions to
problems which interfere with their own effectiveness on
the job. In addition, the circle is often involved in the
actual implementation and monitoring of solutions that the
group has come up with. Since additional knowledge may be
required for these activities, circle members will be trained
by the leader of their Circle in problem-solving techniques.
Group leaders will receive training in these techniques
directly from the facilitator and the RPI support staff.

What Are The Benefits Of A Quality Circle Program?

Quality Circles offer participants the opportunity to use their
own knowledge to solve work methods, quality, safety, and
productivity problems, therefore improving the total OGWD
work environment. At the same time, members can acquire and
develop skills in communications and problem solving which
will prove to be valuable both inside and outside of the circle.
The increased interaction brought about by the circle activities
will also serve to improve communications between employees at
all levels in OGWD. Since Norton intends to remain a profitable
enterprise, it is expected that Quality Circles will improve
the work area, communications, quality, and productivity at
a cost that justifies their existence. In other words, it is
expected that Quality Circles will show a return on the investment of time, energy, and resources that will be contributed
by all those involved.

Source: Reprinted with permission from Norton Company.

Exhibit 6.4 *continued*

```
                              - 2 -

    Five circles are slated to begin operation by the end of the
    year.  New circles will be formed as the original circles
    begin to function more independently, hopefully giving all
    those interested an opportunity to participate.

    More information will be available soon in group meetings and
    on plant bulletin boards.

    The entire Organic management team is committed long term to
    Quality Circles and we look forward to your active participation.

                              Roger J. Dufresne*
                              Plant Manager
                              Organic Grinding Wheel Division

    atk

    *Roger Dufresne was then plant manager, but has since retired.
    His position has not been filled; Lindberg and Hequembourg now
    report directly to the general managers for their product lines.
```

of their own problems instead of coming to their supervisors for everything. Employees would also, he pointed out, come to appreciate what
supervisors had to do to cut through red tape and get things accomplished. Some supervisors found these points persuasive, but others
went along with the program because, as Bianchini noted, "You do
what you're told."

Supervisor Resistance.   Resistance from some supervisors took several forms and arose for different reasons. Some found it difficult to
accept the idea that a worker might have an idea better than their
own. Not all were comfortable with the concept that independent
groups would be suggesting new ways to do things, yet supervisors
would still be the ones held accountable for meeting production and
delivery schedules within the costs budgeted for their areas. Some
supervisors were fearful of losing their authority and said so: "The
way I run my area is the way I want to run it." Bianchini listened,
but let them know QCs were going to happen.

After the program was under way, resistance sometimes appeared in circle behavior. Bianchini described some instances:

*A circle might have wanted to change a routing or do an operation
differently, and the supervisor would use negative comments to steer
them away from it: "That was tried before and it didn't work." Or
maybe he was already working on a project such as improving rejects
on a press; if a QC started to head in that direction, he might cut them
off with, "I'm already working on that." I didn't usually intervene during the meeting—unless a fight broke out—but I'd talk to him after the
meeting and remind him that project choices were up to the members,
not the leader. Then I'd let him handle it at the next meeting, and he
looked good for backing off.*

Structure of the Program

Leadership.   The steering committee decided QC leaders should come from the ranks of the supervisors. Lindberg explained their reasoning:

We wanted to have the leader be a line person, someone who could get things done. We also thought that if the supervisor was the circle leader, he would be more likely to implement their ideas. It was also the best way to meet their concerns about independent groups deciding how things would be done.

This structure built upon the fact that supervisors had all previously received several weeks of supervisory training that could be a foundation for leading the circles.

Program Management.   Bianchini had responsibility for the nuts and bolts of the program. He reported to the steering committee, three of whose members (Hequembourg and Lindberg, the two production managers, and Norm Stotz, head of engineering and production services) assumed primary responsibility for the program. "In a crunch," as Stotz pointed out, "we three are the ones who would have to say, 'This is why we did what we did.' "

Project Approval.   Approval for working on QC projects had to be secured from line management. A simple change required only the supervisor's approval, his writing out a work order, and the group's implementing it. If a supervisor did not approve, the circle could go up to his boss, the general foreman; if he did not approve, they could go to the production manager. A complex project, which required considerable time or money, affected other work areas, or might affect the product, required a more formal presentation to senior division management. Such presentations had to be backed up with solid facts and analysis and usually included the use of visual materials such as flip charts, overhead transparencies, or slides. Similarly, in order to implement their solutions, QCs had to go to line managers. If the proposed action did not affect the production process or product performance, QC members could carry out the proposed action themselves. But if it did, they had to get engineering involved.

The approval process was also more complex if a circle ventured out of its own work area. While most QC operating policies, including GW's, confined projects to a circle's own area, GW did allow projects that crossed departmental lines. Billy Balunis described the process his circle had gone through to deal with air leaks in the piping of compressed gas:

The idea for doing this was suggested by a facilities engineer whom we had invited to a meeting. We decided to do it and presented it to our supervisor. Then Don talked to the general foreman and told him what we wanted to do. We went to the steering committee for permission to go through the plant and study the problem.

Projects

The Process.   Groups brainstormed to generate project ideas and then, through successive rounds of voting, pared their ideas to the ones they wanted to work on. Suggestions and support came from many sources, including the steering committee, the facilitator, and the general foremen, but circle members themselves decided which to pursue. While Bianchini had to counteract the tendency of a few supervisors to be too directive, others hung back, going in the opposite direction so as not to steer project choices.

Projects Chosen.   Initially, most groups started working on small projects that had a high probability of success such as fixing shower heads, improving lighting in their area, or making small layout changes. Bianchini and management encouraged this so members would build up feelings of accomplishment and of being listened to. Many of the ensuing projects were about reduction of waste and salvage of materials and resources, including barrels, paper, water, and air.

Opinion was somewhat divided, however, about the role of QCs with regard to product quality. Balunis reported he had tried to get his circle "more interested in product quality than in salvage, but that's difficult because it means stepping into other people's job areas." Rick Lambert, who had worked in GW for seven years, observed:

Lots of the QC projects are about salvage. It's easy to see the potential savings there because you see the waste happening all day long. But product quality—that's someone else's job. The QCs don't deal with that. I don't feel the environment has really changed because we still have no say in the product.

Paterno conceded there were limits on QC involvement with the product:

We don't want them to fool with the formulas; those are R&D's and engineering's areas. If they wanted to change a bake formula cycle, that would be a borderline area requiring lots of testing to make sure it didn't change or hurt the product. But issues between Molding and Finishing would be fair game.

The Water Conservation Project.   One of the best-known QC projects had greatly reduced the amount of water used to cool both the wheels and the presses in which they were molded. The QC consulted with engineering on ways to adapt a flow control to this application, track the rate of cooling to make sure the wheels were not harmed, and follow press temperatures to make sure the equipment was not being damaged by the change. The circle reduced water usage for ten pieces of equipment from 300 gallons per minute to 57, saving the company $30,000 a year.

The Arbor/Quartz Project.   It was sometimes difficult for members of a department to do their work because of problems that originated in upstream departments. The interfaces between Molding and Finishing were particularly problem-prone. For example, Thin Wheel Finishing had to reject many small wheels whose bushings had been set crookedly by Molding; these same wheels often broke Finishing's fixtures (called *arbors*). The first part of the Finishing QC's solution was to redesign the fixture so as to greatly reduce the cost of breakage.

Reducing the frequency of breakage, however, was not under Finishing's control. The Finishing QC received the grudging consent of Molding to observe its operations. Observation and analysis led the QC to conclude that certain ways molders handled the quartz filler was the cause of the problem. When this analysis was presented to the Molding department, the response, according to Herb Castell, a Finishing Supervisor and QC leader, was

. . . not very good. They felt we were coming in and telling them what to do. They did change their methods some of the time, but not all of the time. When we made a presentation to management, management was very receptive, but it was sticky because it put Molding on the spot. Management then picked it up and worked it back down through the general foreman and the Molding supervisors.

Castell continued:

Interdepartmental projects like this work because management supports them. We go as far up as we need to—the steering committee or the production manager—and he works it back down through the organizational line in the other department. When we just had the suggestion system, if someone said no, that was the end of it.

Presentations.   Once or twice a year, each circle made a formal presentation to management on its work. Presentations were also held whenever the need arose, such as to secure approval for a major project. Paterno, several people pointed out, always came to every presentation, asked good questions, and complimented the circle members on their presentations. He recalled his reactions to the early presentations: "I walked out utterly amazed. They were very professional, using flip charts and statistics, talking about the return on investment of the purchase they wanted to make. And here we had neglected them for years." The steering committee, the division controller, the supervisors, and the general foremen in the circle's area (whether or not involved in circles), and those engineers and others who had provided technical assistance were always invited to presentations and most usually came. Lindberg and Hequembourg said it was a thrill to see how well shop-floor people handled presentations and compared GW's favorably with those of other companies. That, they noted, was also a tribute to Bianchini's coaching.

Where Do QCs Go from Here?

While the QC literature suggested that after several years QCs typically ran their course and petered out, Paterno hadn't seen this happening at GW. He belived the groups would endure, but their roles might evolve. He speculated:

Eventually, I would like to do away with individual incentives and develop a gain-sharing plan in which everyone shares in the cost savings they generate. But before we go to a group incentive, I want to have a team mentality and group dynamics well engrained. I see the QCs as a kind of foundation for this. I can envision a time when groups get together at 7 a. m. to discuss production schedules for the day and then just go off and do it. The QCs wouldn't just be QCs anymore, but would evolve into self-directed work teams.

THE NORTON COMPANY: MANAGING CHANGE AND CHANGING MANAGEMENT (B)

About eight months into the QC program, facilitator Don Bianchini believed it was time to open circle leadership to members. He stated:

I feel it is a test of management. If they are really committed, if they really want employees to be more involved, then they should allow employees to run their own groups. If we give employees more control, they will take more responsibility.

The production managers were not convinced. Hequembourg wondered, "How will the supervisors react? How will they feel about groups they don't control?" Lindberg echoed his sentiments:

Would we be setting up a leader in an area separate from the supervisor? Would someone who isn't a supervisor know how to keep the group effective? Would he know where to go for help?

But Bianchini did not share these concerns:

This is part of the development of people, and people development is one of the stated objectives of the steering committee. If we are really serious about trying to get people to take more responsibility, then we can't say "no" to their assuming circle leadership.

THE NORTON COMPANY: MANAGING CHANGE AND CHANGING MANAGEMENT (C)

When the QC program was kicked off at GW in late 1981, there was no provision for sharing with members any cost savings their projects produced. Nor could QC members use the suggestion system, which remained open to non-QC members. By the following year, Bianchini began to believe a monetary incentive was needed:

> Workers aren't saying anything, but I feel it's making them hold back not to have financial rewards. I want to do something before it becomes an issue. I see a lot of cost savings coming from the projects, but we aren't sharing it with them.

In making this recommendation, Bianchini was going against the conventional wisdom of QC literature and practice. Most QC experts argued that QC rewards should derive from the satisfactions of being listened to, having input and some control over one's work, the sense of achievement from implementing one's ideas, and the recognition and praise from co-workers and management that usually followed.

If the steering committee opted for incentives, they had another issue to grapple with: should the awards be based on one-year savings or multiple-year savings?